250 Music Anecdotes

David Bruce

Published by David Bruce, 2022.

While every precaution has been taken in the preparation of this book, the publisher assumes no responsibility for errors or omissions, or for damages resulting from the use of the information contained herein.

250 MUSIC ANECDOTES

First edition. August 4, 2022.

Copyright © 2022 David Bruce.

ISBN: 979-8201176488

Written by David Bruce.

Table of Contents

Cover Photograph for *250 Music Anecdotes*:
Bruce Dalzell, singer-songwriter

DEDICATED to BRUCE DALZELL

ALBUMS

Austin Sessions (Produced by Carrie Elkin)

Kiss of the Muse

Live From Home

My Athens Past

The Song of Flying

For 35 years, Bruce Dalzell has emceed Ohio University's Open-Mic Night in the Front Room at Baker University Center.

For many years, he has also hosted the Tuesday Night Songwriter Circle at Ohio University.

Singer-Songwriter Circle

https://www.youtube.com/watch?v=sgGJ0maiJtw

Bruce Dalzell on Spotify

https://open.spotify.com/search/bruce%20dalzell

Bruce Dalzell on Spotify #2

https://open.spotify.com/artist/
4sYDpj0RF3MAmHluwz8I0w

Bruce Dalzell on YouTube

https://www.youtube.com/channel/
UCDciWlmMAm5FnsP6nMRpTkg

Bruce Dalzell TOPIC

https://www.youtube.com/channel/
UCQDeJcuvWusrxDdtmjlGMKw

BRUCE DALZELL: "MY BABY SCARES ME"

She's a bottle of mescal on a Tuesday night

She's a bronco-bull rider all dressed in white

She's a fine-glass jewel box full of dynamite

My baby scares me, umm, my baby scares me

She's driving a Mercedes-Benz with your eyes closed

She's doing the tango in a bed of roses

She's skydiving wearing no clothes

My baby scares me, ooh, my baby scares me

She's walking in a thunderstorm in a tinfoil hat
She is skinny-dipping with a Siamese cat
She's strolling in a biker bar with a cricket bat
My baby scares me, ooh, my baby scares me
She's got me stepping me up to my fear
Got me forgetting all I know
She's got me laughing through my tears
She's got me eating fish with a nice Bordeaux
When the audience is silent, she sings along loud
Looks at me with desire even in a crowd
In this cookie-cutter world the woman makes me proud
My baby scares me, I kind of like that
My baby scares me.
Lyrics copyright by Bruce Dalzell

Chapter 1: From Advertising to Clothing Advertising

• Mary Garden was a celebrity soprano and diva, and people enjoyed spreading gossip about her — which is a form of advertising for a diva. One story was about the long golden blond hair she needed to play the role of Mélisande. Gossipers said that she sent people throughout France to find a woman with long golden blond hair. When the right woman was found, Ms. Garden paid her hundreds of dollars for her hair and had it made into a wig. Another story involved a donkey that appeared with her in one of Massenet's operas. Gossipers said that Ms. Garden had trained the donkey to look interested and prick up its ears whenever she sang but to look bored and let its ears droop whenever anyone else sang![1]

 • One of Ramones lead singer Joey Ramone's early jobs was passing out advertising fliers for West Village massage parlors; however, he wasn't a good employee. He used to throw away the fliers and use his pay to buy himself beers instead of doing the work he was supposed to be doing. When Joey was 13, he taught his mother how to smoke marijuana. She used to let him and his brother smoke marijuana in the basement because she worried that they would be arrested if they smoked it outside the house.[2]

Advice

 • Even as a kid, Debbie Gibson loved music and soon knew that she wanted to be a singer and musician. When she was a two-year-old toddler, she wanted a present: a guitar. However, because her hands were too little to play a guitar, her parents got her a ukulele instead. When Diane, Debbie's mother, bought a piano later, Diane was not able to learn to play it. Instead, the Gibson daughters, including Debbie, played the piano for hours each day. Debbie remembers, "It got so bad, especially after [the fourth and youngest Gibson daughter]

Denise started, we had to get two pianos. Between the four of us, there was at least eight hours of practicing a day." At age four, Debbie played a song that she had learned by ear: "Billy, Don't Be a Hero," by Bo Donaldson and the Heywoods. Debbie wrote her very first song while she was in kindergarten. Her teacher gave the little students some advice that Debbie turned into a song: "Make Sure You Always Know Your Classroom." (Her sisters had to write down the lyrics she had created because Debbie didn't know how to write yet.) Also while she was in kindergarten, Debbie made an Easter bonnet along with the other children. But Debbie went home and created another Easter bonnet that she wore to school the next day. Her teacher, Mrs. Murray (no first name given), remembers that it was "three times the size of the hats the class had made. And she'd pasted everything she could find on it — everything, it seemed, but the kitchen sink!"[3]

• On the WWW is the "Bikini Kill Archive" in which fans of Kathleen Hanna's riot grrrl group Bikini Kill are invited to do this: "Please add your Bikini Kill story to this blog! It can be totally off the top of your head and doesn't need to be fancy. Maybe it's your reaction to a song we wrote, something weird that happened at one of our shows, a personal anecdote or just WHATEVER. Feel free to send images too!" A young woman who calls herself Harriet Doorstop wrote about discovering Bikini Kill's music as a 14-year-old growing up in rural southeastern Minnesota. Ms. Doorstop wrote, "All I ever remember doing after that was smiling. Smiling as I read about Bikini Kill, Sleater-Kinney, Hole, and Bratmobile. Smiling as I listened to Rebel Girl on youtube. Smiling as I ordered an album called Pussy Whipped ('Pussy Whipped'??? Holy sh[*]t!) off the internet. Smiling as I started learning how to play the guitar.... Smiling was never something that I did a whole lot before. I never felt like I was entitled to. Now I know that I am, though." She also wrote that she intended to start a band. Of course, Ms. Hanna reads the Bikini Kill Archive. She posted this message for Ms. Doorstop: "Your band is gonna change the world. Don't delay, start it now!!! xoxoKathleen." Kathleen Hanna could very well be right. It could happen.[4]

Alcohol

• Sam Andrew played guitar in the bands Big Brother and the Holding Company and the Kozmic Blues, both of which backed up vocalist Janis Joplin. He remembers that a critic once wrote, "Janis Joplin has true melisma in her singing." She looked up the word "melisma" and discovered that it was a technique used in much Gospel and choir music. According to the online Free Dictionary, melisma is "A passage of several notes sung to one syllable of text, as in Gregorian chant." Mr. Andrew remembers, "After she had learned what it meant, Janis didn't stop saying the word 'melisma' for a week. That's the way she was about praise. She couldn't get enough of it." Not everyone enjoyed her singing. Early in her career, the police showed up as she was rehearsing with Big Brother because they had received a report about a screaming woman. Of course, some of Janis' life was wild and crazy; after all, she died of an accidental heroin overdose and alcohol. She was often photographed with a bottle of Southern Comfort in her hand, and she frequently mentioned the brand in interviews. She told the *New York Times Magazine*, "I had the chick in my manager's office photostat every god*amn clipping that ever had me mentioning Southern Comfort, and I sent them to the company, and they sent me a whole lotta money. How could anybody in their right mind want me for their image? Oh, man, that was the best hustle I ever pulled — can you imagine getting paid for passing out for two years?" In addition to giving Janis money, the company gave her a lynx coat. Janis also told the *New York Times Magazine*, "Man, I'd rather have ten years of superhypermost than live to be seventy sitting in some godd*mn chair watching TV."[5]

• One winter while Walter Damrosch was conducting at the Metropolitan Opera, he and his family stayed at the Cambridge Hotel on Fifth Avenue, where their waiter, Roberto, taught them about hospitality and wine. For example, he criticized a host who had ordered only one bottle of wine. Roberto said, "There are five of them, and he orders the dinner. Then I show him the wine card. He orders *one* bottle — one bottle for five! I fool him. I open another bottle. I shame him into behaving like a gentleman!" Later, after a performance in which Lillian Nordica had sung a fine performance of Elsa in Wagner's *Lohengrin*, Mr. Damrosch gave a late supper party. His daughter Gretchen was supposed to be asleep in bed, but she stayed awake and counted the popping of corks. She remembered, "There were eight people, and so far only one cork had popped. Bing, a second one. Good. Was two for eight better than one for five? Bang, and a third bottle was opened. I lay back greatly relieved, and relaxed. I must tell Roberto at breakfast. Nothing wrong with my father!"[6]

• Glen Campbell has many souvenirs from his long career in show business, including many photographs of himself with many notabilities. He also has a souvenir from his drinking days. He had given up drinking, but during a relapse he was stopped for driving drunk — and for a hit-and-run accident. He then proceeded to knee a police officer in the thigh. As a result, he spent 10 days in jail while wearing pink underwear. Glen's wife, Kim, says, "Sheriff Joe Arpaeo from Phoenix, Arizona, is famous for making all the inmates wear pink underwear, and I have a pair signed by the sheriff. Glen straightened up after that." Glen agrees: "Yep. I finally got broke from sucking eggs, as they say."[7]

• As a young woman, Courtney Love, who was later the lead singer of Hole, wanted to marry fellow musician Rozz Rezabek, and she occasionally proposed to him. One night, they were sitting in a train boxcar and drinking champagne, and again she proposed to him. The two, however, found out that they were not alone. They had woken up a wino who grumbled, "Oh, go ahead. Marry her."[8]

• Composer Arthur Sullivan enjoyed drinking. In fact, one day he was so inebriated that he found it difficult to tell his house from the other houses on his street. Therefore, he kicked the metal shoe scraper on each top step he came to. Eventually, he murmured, "E flat," then went to his door and let himself in.[9]

• CBGB's is well known as a venue for early performances by such bands as the Ramones, Talking Heads, and Blondie. People under age 18 could get in to hear the bands, but their hands were stamped "Nobooze foyouz."[10]

Animals

• Is this the kind of thing you would expect to hear from a musician? "I got a job working with great tits. [...] So I was counting great tits, measuring them, weighing them. I've worked with great tits and white-breasted thrashers." In a way, yes. In a way, no. The speaker is Brian Briggs, the frontman for Stornoway, a Britain nu-folk band, and he is talking about birds of the non-human variety. He has a Ph.D. in zoology: "Ducks, actually." One of his jobs in zoology was discovering "what [ducks] like and what they don't like, in lakes and reservoirs in southwest London. And the answer is they like food and they don't like waterskiing."[11]

• In 1890, while preparing to make his London debut at St. James' Hall, pianist Ignacy Paderewski suffered from stage fright. Fortunately, when he sat down on the piano bench, the theater cat walked out and jumped on his lap. The audience laughed, and Mr. Paderewski relaxed. He played magnificently, and the cat kept on sitting on his lap. Of course, Mr. Paderewski became a world-famous musician, and he gave credit to the cat that had cured his stage fright.[12]

Audiences

• Hardcore group Black Flag sometimes played shows for very few people. In 1982, Black Flag played a show in Oklahoma City, Oklahoma, for two, or at most five people, who sat far away, in the back. Henry Rollins, lead singer, was mad, and he complained about the lack of audience just before Black Flag went on stage to perform. Fortunately, Black Flag bassist Chuck Dukowski talked to him, and in Mr. Rollins' words, "straightened me out on a few things." Mr. Dukowski taught him "that even though there were only a few people there, it didn't matter. They were there to see us, and that was good enough." Mr. Rollins adds, "He said that you never pull a bullsh*t attitude on stage, and you always play your *ss off or don't play at all." Mr. Rollins remembers the show that Black Flag played that night. He says, "I played my *ss off that night." Mr. Rollins sings, performs spoken-word concerts, and writes. He says, "I am a guy who used to work at an ice cream store in Washington, D.C. I am of average intelligence. There's nothing special about me. If I can get this far, I would be very surprised if you couldn't get at least twice as far. F**k them. Keep your blood clean, your body lean, and your mind sharp."[13]

• People sometimes cough during a performance of an opera or other music, although that is rude. A friend of conductor William Christie once attended a chamber-music recital at Carnegie, and in front of him was a cougher. At an appropriate moment, he asked her, "Couldn't you be a bit quieter?" She replied, "Young man, I've been coughing here for 40 years." Mr. Christie has himself told a person behind him, "Have you noticed that my orchestra — and often there are 60 of them — don't cough? Why do you cough?" Of course, some coughs are OK. Mr. Christie says, "When I stop playing music and hear this chorus of coughing, you realize that people have been making an effort" not to cough during the music. And a singer once told interviewer Joshua Jampol "that during lieder concerts, the audience coughed when he finished a song because they had been so concentrated that they'd forgotten to breathe or swallow." By the way, Mr. Christie's friend Simon Rattle once became so annoyed by the ringing of cell phones during a concert that he stopped the concert and walked off the stage. Then he returned to the stage and told the audience, "If that happens again, I'll do it again."[14]

• Jim Peterik wrote "Vehicle," the biggest hit of the rock group Ides of March. Mr. Peterik still performs the song, sometimes in unlikely places. In San Francisco, he saw a musician busking for spare change on the street. He listened to a song, gave the busker some spare change, and then said that he played guitar. The busker handed over his guitar, and Mr. Peterik played and sang "Vehicle." Apparently, the busker enjoyed the song, because he gave back to Mr. Peterik the spare change that Mr. Peterik had given to him. Of course, Mr. Peterik has been around for many years, and he has known legends. When he was 20 years old, he opened for the Allman Brothers. While the Allmans were on stage, Duane Allman asked the audience for some coke, so Mr. Peterik ran on stage with a can of Coca-Cola. He did not understand why the audience laughed.[15]

• Audience members will often applaud vigorously if they know that a big-name vocalist is singing, but if they do not know that a big-name vocalist is singing, they will often remain quiet. Albert Reiss was a competent tenor, but he lacked a big name although one evening he did not lack laryngitis. Enrico Caruso, who had perhaps the biggest name among tenors, offered to sing Arlecchino's arietta for him while he mouthed the words, and Mr. Caruso also bet Mr. Reiss that no one in the audience would know that he was doing so. Mr. Caruso sang for Mr. Reiss and no one went wild, but the next time Mr. Caruso sang and the audience knew that he was singing, the audience went wild.[16]

• During the 1992 Reading Festival, rain poured down and formed mud — lots of mud. A feisty audience began throwing gobs of mud at the performers on stage. Members of the grunge band Mudhoney put down their instruments and began throwing gobs of mud back at the audience. Mark Arm, vocalist for Mudhoney, taunted the British mud-throwers: "You guys can't throw. You're used to playing soccer and kicking balls with your feet." At that moment, a big gob of mud splattered his face. Later, Mr. Arm joked, "That'll learn me. Never taunt an armed audience."[17]

Autographs

• When Irene Daye, the singer for Gene Krupa's band, retired, Anita O'Day took over for her. One day, someone asked her for her autograph, which she was happy to give. Unfortunately, after the person had gotten her autograph and the two had parted, Ms. O'Day heard the autograph-seeker mutter, "Aw, she ain't Irene!" Ms. O'Day then looked back, and she saw the autograph-seeker tear out a page from the autograph book and throw it away.[18]

• Band leader Doc Severinsen, most famous as the band leader on Johnny Carson's *Tonight Show*, and his wife, Emily, were fighting and screaming in a hotel room when he noticed a paper being slipped under the door. The paper was a note from some people requesting an autograph. Doc and Emily opened the door and signed some autographs, and then they closed the door and started fighting and screaming again.[19]

Automobiles

• Following the wartime austerity of World War II and the rise of making much money playing rock and roll, some British performers began — of course — spending money on cars. British jazz musician George Melly and early British rocker Tommy Steele met backstage once, and Mr. Steele learned that Mr. Melly did not have a car. Mr. Melly remembers, "He looked at me with the sort of pity usually reserved for the badly deformed."[20]

• Wynonie Harris was a rhythm and blues star of the 1940s and 1950s who made a lot of money and spent a lot of money. He bought two Cadillacs and hired two chauffeurs, and people used to go out on the sidewalk at 4 a.m. when he left the Baby Grand in Harlem after a performance just to see which Cadillac he would choose to ride home in.[21]

Bathrooms

• Lucas Silveira was born female, but later he became the transgender guitarist and singer of the music group the Cliks. Even when he was a little girl, he knew that he wanted to be a boy. He wanted his mother to cut his hair short, and whenever he had to wear a dress, he screamed. However, one very happy experience occurred when he was seven or eight years old and living in a Portuguese village. He says, "My parents took me to this festival. I was playing with a bunch of kids, and these two little girls I was playing with thought I was a boy — so I just went along with it. They were like, 'We need to go to the bathroom,' and I was like, 'Well, I need to go to the bathroom, too.' And they went, 'Well, you're a boy, you can pee over there' — up against the wall. And I literally pretended to pee up against the wall because, hey, that's what boys do. But I went with it. And I remember how happy I was in that moment."[22]

• Tribe 8 is an all-lesbian punk bank from San Francisco. One problem that they run into while on tour is getting bathroom privileges — sometimes when they go into the women's bathroom women will tell them that they are in the wrong bathroom. Their appearance really does sometimes confuse people about their gender. Vocalist Lynn Breedlove says, "Little old ladies will come in the women's room behind us, and then they'll pop out and look at the sign on the door." Once, an old man followed them into the men's room because he thought that they were men. Ms. Breedlove says, "He *jumped* out." Rhythm guitarist Lynn Feather has actually lifted her shirt to show that she has breasts and to prove that she is in the correct bathroom. The band wrote a song about this problem; of course, the song is titled "Wrong Bathroom."[23]

• Roy Henderson once started practicing some vocal exercises in an empty cloakroom, thinking that no one could hear him. However, he was startled to hear a toilet flushing, followed shortly by a man coming out of a door at one end of the cloakroom. "I'm extremely sorry," Mr. Henderson said. "I hope I didn't disturb you." The man replied, "On the contrary, I found it quite helpful."[24]

Big Breaks

• British pop musician Billy Bragg contributed to his big break. His regular job was working at a 24-hour gas station when he heard radio deejay John Peel say on the air that he wanted a mushroom biryani so badly that he would do anything for it. Within 30 minutes Mr. Bragg appeared at the radio station with a mushroom biryani. What was the "anything" that Mr. Peel ended up doing for the mushroom biryani? He played on the air Mr. Bragg's "The Milkman of Human Kindness." These days, the music industry is changing because people are downloading music instead of buying CDs. Mr. Bragg is hopeful that this era of change will work out OK for the musicians. He points out, "You only need to find 5,000 people willing to pay you £10 a year to make you give up your day job."[25]

• A big break early in Barbra Streisand's career came in the theater when at age 19 she auditioned for and won the supporting role of Miss Marmelstein, who sings one three-minute song in the musical *I Can Get It for You Wholesale*. At the end of her first audition — which went well — for the part, Ms. Streisand pleaded, "Will somebody call me, please! Even if I don't get the part, just call!" Elliott Gould, the lead actor in the play, did call her, told her who he was, said, 'You were brilliant!' — and hung up. Of course, Ms. Streisand's song in the musical became a show-stopper. (By the way, Mr. Gould became Ms. Streisand's first husband.)[26]

• Conductor James Conlon was ready for his big break when it came. He was studying conducting at Julliard, and a famous conductor — Thomas Schippers — was supposed to conduct *La Bohème* there, but Mr. Schippers became ill and cancelled. Mr. Conlon rehearsed the orchestra while the school looked for another conductor. At the time, Maria Callas was giving master classes, and the president of Julliard asked Ms. Callas her opinion of Mr. Conlon. Mr. Conlon says, "Callas listened to me rehearse for about 15 minutes, walked out and told him, 'There's your man; he's got a great future.'" And Mr. Conlon conducted the first of many successes.[27]

Birthdays

• Two abilities led to Corey Glover becoming the singer of funk-metal band Living Colour: the ability to sing "Happy Birthday" and the ability to show up for a gig. Mr. Glover attended a friend's birthday party, which Living Colour guitarist Vernon Reid also attended. Requested to sing "Happy Birthday," Mr. Glover obliged, and Mr. Reid told him, "We [Mr. Reid and his sister] like the way you sing." A couple of months later, he called Mr. Glover and said, "I'm looking for a singer for my band." One other singer was also in the running, but a few more months after Mr. Glover's audition, he got another call from Mr. Reid, who told him, "Our singer can't make the gig. Can you come down and do it?" Mr. Glover responded, "Sure. No problem. Whatever. Do I get paid for the gig? I do? All right, cool. I'll go." That's the way Mr. Glover became the band's singer and started performing in interesting places and winning Grammy Awards for songs such as "Cult of Personality" and "Glamour Boys." He says about his first gig with Living Colour, "So it was actually my first time performing at CBGB's, which was a big enough deal for me anyway. It looks like a hole in the wall, it smells like a hole in the wall, it is a hole in the wall, but it's amazing. Well, it's not there anymore, but it was amazing. So that was my first gig, and I've been in the band ever since. The guy never came back."[28]

• The music and image of heavy-metal band Black Sabbath included references to black magic, but the band did not take it seriously. Once, lead singer Ozzy Osbourne found some Satanists conducting a black-magic ritual outside his hotel room. He responded by first blowing out their candles and then singing "Happy Birthday."[29]

Books

• When Robert Louis Stevenson, author of *Treasure Island*, was sailing in the South Seas, he used to dictate stories to his stepson, who typed them. South Sea natives observed this procedure, then explained it by saying that Mr. Stevenson was singing and his stepson was accompanying him on a musical instrument. By the way, when Mr. Stevenson was sailing in the South Seas, he stopped at Sydney, Australia. He went to the Victoria Hotel, but because he was rudely treated there, he immediately switched to a different hotel. The next day, the newspapers ran front-page stories about the visit of famous author Robert Louis Stevenson, so the Victoria Hotel management visited him to ask him to move back into the Victoria Hotel. He declined to do so.[30]

• Björk's first boyfriend owned 10,000 books — and he read them. Because he was well read, he was always ready to help Björk find exactly what she wanted to read. For example, she would tell him, "Listen, I want to read something that's kind of, like, hairy and dangerous with a nice female character." And he would get a book, hand it to her, and say, "Here you go." Björk has a collection of books, although it may not what you think it would be. When she enjoys reading a book, she gives it away. Then she buys another copy and gives that one away, too. She says, "So I haven't got any books I like — only those I don't."[31]

Children

• Some famous composers had interesting experiences as children: 1) As a boy, Johann Sebastian Bach loved music and wanted to study a book of difficult music that his brother, the organist Johann Christoph, owned. Unfortunately, his brother would not allow him to borrow the book because he felt that it was too difficult for his young brother. Therefore, Johann Sebastian "borrowed" the book each night without permission, took it to his bedroom, and copied it. 2) Before he was seven years old, George Frederic Handel smuggled a clavichord into the attic so he could play it for hours at a time. 3) As a boy, Franz Joseph Haydn marched in a band in a parade. His job was to play the drum, but he was too small to carry it. To solve the problem, his teacher strapped the drum on the back of another person, and young Joseph walked behind him and played the drum. As an adult, he composed the

Surprise Symphony, which contains a loud, unexpected chord during a period of quiet music. Why did he do this? He explained, "To make the ladies jump." 4) As a boy, Franz Peter Schubert made things difficult — in a good way — for his music teacher Michael Holzer, who told Franz' father, "Whenever I want to teach him something new, I find he already knows it." 5) What is it like to be the son of a famous father and the father of a famous son? The father of Abraham Mendelssohn was Moses Mendelssohn, a famous philosopher; the son of Abraham Mendelssohn was Felix Mendelssohn, a famous composer. People tended to refer to him in terms of his famous relatives. Abraham Mendelssohn once said, "Formerly I was the son of my father; now I am the father of my son." The young Felix Mendelssohn was fortunate enough to be invited to spend two weeks at the home of the great poet Johann von Goethe. Fanny, Felix' sister, was jealous and wrote him in a letter, "When you are with Goethe, open your eyes and ears wide; and after you come home, if you can't repeat every word that fell from his mouth, I will have nothing more to do with you!" In a letter to Fanny, Felix wrote about Goethe, "The amount of sound in his voice is wonderful, and he can shout like ten thousand warriors." 6) Before he was 15 years old, Richard Wagner wrote a tragedy that was influenced by Shakespeare. So many people died in the tragedy that in order to have a fifth act he had to bring the characters back as ghosts. 7) Edvard Grieg's first teacher was his mother, who would listen to him play the piano as she cooked and would make comments as needed: "For shame, Edvard. F sharp, F sharp — not F." People loved Edvard. As an adult composer, he had a studio — a cabin — built. Unfortunately, he discovered that it was too near the highway, and so he held a "moving bee." Friends came over, picked up the cabin, and moved it deeper into the woods.[32]

• Stevie Wonder's father was a joker. He told his children, who spent the early part of their life in Saginaw, Michigan, which was very cold in the winter, that Saginaw was located only 12 miles from the

North Pole. Mr. Wonder said, "I believed that for a long time." Mr. Wonder himself is a joker. Although he is blind, he once told *Jet* magazine that he wanted to judge a beauty contest. Once, when he entered someone's living room he moved his head from side to side and said, "Wow, really nice place you got here." When he was young, his friends and family played a game with him. They would throw a coin on a table, and he would listen to it and identify it: "That's a dime" or "That's a quarter." He did have difficulty distinguishing between the sound of a nickel and the sound of a penny. When he was young, another joke he played was on his friend Dionne Warwick, who had a red dress that the Shirelles hated, so the Shirelles enlisted Mr. Wonder's help. He was able to identify her by the perfume she wore and so he would greet her. She asked him, "Hello, baby, how are you today?" He replied, "Dionne, I don't like that red dress." Ms. Warwick said, "It scared me, because I know he's blind and there's no way in the world this kid can see this dress, but if he didn't like it I'm takin' it off. I never wore that dress again. It took two or three years before the Shirelles finally broke down and told me what they'd done." Mr. Wonder once said, "Being physically blind is no crime, but being spiritually blind is a serious handicap."[33]

• The father of piano prodigy Clara Wieck, who married composer Robert Schumann in 1840, was Frederick Wieck, and he could be a hard man to deal with. When Clara was a child, he once thought that she had played a piano piece poorly, and he tore up the music and called her "lazy, careless, disorderly, stubborn, and disobedient." He also refused to let her play her favorite pieces of music for weeks and returned the music to her only after she promised to be good. She had high standards for piano playing. When she was still a 10-year-old child but playing concerts professionally, she once was given a poor piano to play at a concert. After she had finished, the members of the audience applauded, but she stood up and told them, "Now you are clapping, and I know that I played badly." As she said that, some tears ran down her cheeks. When she was 12 years old, the famous German writer Johann von Goethe said about her, "She plays with as much strength as six boys." She was born in 1819 and lived in a sexist age. In 1879, when she was a widow, she taught at an important music conservatory in Frankfurt, whose director wrote about her, "With the exception of Madame Schumann, there is no woman and there will not be any women employed in the Conservatory. As for Madame Schumann, I count her as a man."[34]

• When Joan Oliver Goldsmith, a volunteer singer in a chorus, was around seven years old, her younger sister made a 25-cent bet with her that she would not be able to go an entire day without singing. (In 1958, 25 cents would buy two Superman comic books.) In the afternoon, Joan forgot the bet and started to sing, "Thumbelina, Thumbelina, tiny little thing." The adult Joan decided to switch from singing soprano to alto in the chorus. When other people in the chorus asked her about the change, she replied, "Yes, I've switched from soprano to alto. I've also moved from St. Paul to Minneapolis. I can't think of any more fundamental changes short of a sex-change operation." By the way, this is a joke that singers sometimes tell among themselves: "How many sopranos does it take to screw in a light bulb? [...] Three. One to screw it in. One to pull the ladder out from under her. And one to say, 'I could have done it better than that!'"[35]

• Country singer LeAnn Rimes' father, Wilbur, learned early not to underestimate her talent. When she was six years old, she entered a talent contest, at which she sang the song "Getting to Know You" well. However, her father saw that the other contestants were twice as old as LeAnn, so he figured that the judges would not vote for her. Therefore, he went hunting instead of waiting for the results of the talent contest. When he got home, LeAnn was carrying into their home the first-place trophy. Obviously, LeAnn started singing early in her life. Her mother, Belinda, remembers her sleeping in the family car, waking up and singing a song and then going to sleep again. And as a professional singer, the young LeAnn would play with her Barbies in her dressing room until it was time to go on stage and sing.[36]

• Barbara Mandrell is the oldest of three daughters. At age six, she liked being the only child, but then her parents had another daughter. Her father knew that Barbara liked being the only child, so when he brought her new sister home, he pretended that the hospital had given them the wrong baby: "This is not our baby; it has black hair and it's just not ours, and I'm going to flush it down the toilet." He went into the bathroom, and young Barbara pleaded with him, "No, give me the baby! She's my baby!" He came out of the bathroom with the baby and let Barbara hold her, and Barbara stopped being jealous and started loving her baby sister.[37]

• The three brothers who make up the music group Hanson — Ike, Taylor, and Zac Hanson — started singing and making music together when they were very young. Often, they would ignore a chore such as washing and drying the dishes so that they could create a new song together. No problem. Their parents would happily listen to them sing the new song — then make them wash and dry the dishes. By the way, this is the dumbest question these three brothers have ever been asked: "How did you guys meet?"[38]

• Susan Rotolo was at one time Bob Dylan's girlfriend, and his and her photograph appears on the cover of his album *Freewheelin' Bob Dylan*. The relationship didn't last, and she married another man and had a son with him. One day, at Tower Records she saw the album and for fun she asked her young son, "Do you know who is in that picture?" He looked and said, "That's you, Mommy." She says, "It was cute."[39]

• In the 19th century, when singer Emma Abbott was a little girl, she was intrigued to hear about bouquets of flowers being thrown to a prima donna on a stage. However, she worried that the prima donna would fall off if the stage should start going. Fortunately, her father was able to explain to her the difference between a stage and a stagecoach.[40]

Christmas

• Guy Lombardo and eight other teenagers, including his brothers, arrived in the United States from Canada with plans to make it big as musicians. They got a small job in Cleveland, Ohio, and then jobs became hard to find. On Christmas Eve, they were unhappy. They had also decided to go home — defeated. But a knock sounded on the door. They opened it, and the parents of all the teenagers were there. The teenagers had been writing letters with fake cheerfulness, and their parents had seen through the fake cheerfulness. Their parents spent Christmas Eve and Christmas with them. A very successful Guy Lombardo wrote much later, "Their very presence, their cheering words, their show of faith in our ability to succeed was exactly the tonic we needed. We decided not to give up, but to keep trying. And the breaks finally came our way."[41]

• In 1986, after the pop duo Wham!, one of whose hits was "Wake Me Up Before You Go-Go," had split up, George Michael did not have a concert to sing at over the Christmas season. Feeling the desire to sing in public, but not wanting to be recognized, he wore a wig as he and some friends sang carols and popular songs — but not Wham! songs — in English pubs. He discovered that the pub customers liked the Beatles songs best, and he and his friends made £7½ in tips. By the way, when Mr. Michael and Andrew Ridgeley first became famous as Wham!, fans could still look up Andrew's address in the telephone book. Sometimes, teenaged girls went to his home and Andrew's father gave them souvenirs: Andrew's socks.[42]

• When Lady Gaga was a child, her father gave her a special Christmas gift: *The Bruce Springsteen Songbook*. Her favorite song was "Thunder Road," and her father promised that if she learned to play that song, the family would take out a loan and buy a grand piano. After she became famous, Lady Gaga remembered, "So it was the hardest thing for me." The song was hard to learn, and she had trouble understanding the songbook. She said, however, "I just started reading it and eventually got it down." True to his word, her father bought a baby grand. Her family still has it. In 2010, Lady Gaga won two Grammies. She wrote on Twitter, "My dad put them on the piano I studied on for 14 yrs."[43]

• Wendell Corey (1914-1968), an American actor who appeared in such films as *Sorry, Wrong Number* and *Rear Window*, remembers his most memorable Christmas. In 1956, his oldest daughter, Robin, had been in bed for six months after falling ill with rheumatic fever. In September her doctors even thought that she would die. Because it was Christmas, her doctors allowed her to get out of bed and join the family. Wendell and his wife, Alice, prayed for a blessing. Robin came downstairs, put on a Harry Belafonte record, and danced. And after Christmas she continued to grow stronger, and in 1963, when Mr. Corey wrote about her, she was completely healthy — and the Corey family were big fans of Harry Belafonte.[44]

• Denise Jackson, wife of country and western singer Alan Jackson, knows how to give good Christmas gifts. For Christmas 1996, she gave her mother a mink coat (Alan gave his mother a mink coat, too). Denise says, "And my mom opened it and she was just prancing around like a teenager and was just thrilled." Denise's sister-in-law asked Denise's mother where she would wear the fur coat, and she replied that she was going to the local steak house — a restaurant somewhat classier than a Dairy Queen. By the way, one Christmas Denise gave her husband a car that looked familiar to him. He said, "That looks just like the 1955 Thunderbird I built [restored] in high school." Denise replied, "It is."[45]

• On Christmas night of 1987, Jam Master Jay of Run-DMC fame was driving his Jeep when a car driving on the wrong side of the street hit him. Unconscious, he was taken to the emergency room, and he stayed at the hospital for a few days. Exactly one year later, he came out of the Tunnel nightclub in Manhattan. Unfortunately, a fight broke out between some other people. A man fired some shots, and Jay was shot in the leg. He ended up in the same emergency room where he had been taken a year previously. The same doctor and the same nurse were on duty, and they looked at Jay and said, "Jay! Not you again!"[46]

• Heidi May is a woman of wit and intelligence. Her Christmas present to her boss, Henry Rollins, former singer of Black Flag, leader of the Rollins Band, spoken-word artist, occasional actor, and author, was a T-shirt on the back of which are the words "HEIDI RULES!!!" (By the way, Heidi is married, but not to Henry. She is a long-time employee of Henry's company, 2.13.61. Also by the way, Henry was born on February 13, 1961.)[47]

Clothing

• Anita O'Day helped change the way that female singers dressed in the 1940s. Usually, they wore nice dresses, but that can cause problems: 1) good dresses can be expensive, and 2) keeping dresses clean and looking good during life on the road can be difficult. Once, jazz vocalist Anita O'Day bought a floral-print dress at a thrift store, but after wearing the dress during a performance in a club without air conditioning, she discovered why the dress had been so reasonably priced. Ms. O'Day had perspired — a lot — and the perspiration had caused the ink in the floral-print dress to tattoo her body. Her skin now looked like a flower garden. Because of that mishap, she went to bandleader Gene Krupa and said that she would continue to wear dresses at fancy venues, but she would like to wear easier-to-keep-looking-nice shirts, skirts, and band jackets in other venues. Mr. Krupa said that was OK with him, and soon other female vocalists dressed like Ms. O'Day.[48]

• At a show in London, Roy Stride, lead singer of Scouting for Girls, sang the song "1+1=3," which is about an unplanned pregnancy. The lyrics include the line "Take off your clothes and come to bed," and when he sang the line, six males in the balcony stripped off their clothing and flung it onto the stage. Mr. Stride says, "I was nearly knocked out by a shoe." He adds, "When I wrote the song, I honestly never considered fans would take the lyrics literally. Greg [Churchouse], our guitarist, says he suspected there might be some stripping. He blames me for being confronted by six bare male butts when he walked into our dressing room after the show. I was just glad the guys had come to collect their clothes. I was worried they'd go home naked."[49]

• People should be able to wear pretty much whatever they want to, as long as the clothing covers the essentials, but other people can be judgmental. Ani DiFranco started her career as a musician with a look that included a shaved head and big boots. Later, she decided she wanted hair and a pretty dress. But she remembers the first time she walked out onstage in a dress — she heard young women screaming, "Sellout!"[50]

Chapter 2: From Comedians to Fame

Comedians

• Comedian Jack Benny played the violin, and many of his friends were famous musicians. Jascha Heifetz, Gregor Piatagorsky, Leonard Pennario, and Mr. Benny once were at the home of Joan, Mr. Benny's daughter. Mr. Benny sat in a chair, which made a noise, and Mr. Heifetz immediately said, "E flat." Mr. Benny, however, said, "E natural." Joan went to the piano, played E flat, and Mr. Benny sat down in the chair again. The noise it made was E flat. Mr. Benny was happy to have been proven wrong and happy that Mr. Heifetz' renowned perfect pitch had been proven right once more. By the way, when Mr. Benny celebrated his 80th birthday, movie director Billy Wilder gave him the perfect gift: two copies of the book *Life Begins at Forty*.[51]

• Steve Martin is an accomplished comedian, actor, author, and bluegrass banjo player. In 2010, he won a Best Bluegrass Album Grammy for *The Crow*, his first album of original bluegrass songs. In 2011, he recorded another album of original bluegrass songs, with help from friends. The Dixie Chicks sang his song "You," which is about a past relationship. Paul McCartney sang the lead on the song "On Best Love," which is about happiness in a marriage. Originally, Sir Paul thought that he would be singing backup, but then he heard Mr. Martin's singing and told him, "You know, when you said you were a terrible singer, I thought you were being humble, but you weren't."[52]

• Before Johnny Carson was a really big star, he went to Jilly's bar and restaurant, the hangout of Frank Sinatra, who was a really big star. When Frank walked in, Jilly's went quiet. Frank was king there — and everywhere else, too. Johnny, however, said in an exasperated voice, "Frank, I told you 11:30." Johnny was present for the launch of the rocket that took Neil Armstrong to the Moon. He was impressed as the rocket took off and quietly said, "Jesus Christ." In the seat ahead of him was a representative of the Vatican, who turned around and said, "Name-dropper!"[53]

• Comedian Joe E. Lewis' signature song was "Sam, You Made the Pants Too Long," which meant he had to sing it at almost every performance. One day, he came out on stage wearing earmuffs and told the audience, "Ladies and gentlemen. Tonight I'm going to sing 'Sam, You Made the Pants Too Long,' but I'm wearing these earmuffs because I'll be godd*mned if I'm going to listen to it again."[54]

Composers

• Hans Pfitzner, composer of the opera *Palestrina*, went to a German town for an event and stayed in a small hotel. He got up early and started composing, but at 7:30 a.m. workers began to break up with a drill the street outside his hotel room. Mr. Pfitzner opened his window and shouted, "Quiet! Pfitzner lives here!" By the way, Mr. Pfitzner once asked the young Hans Hotter to sing, with himself as the accompanist, some of Mr. Pfitzner's songs and some ballads by Carl Loewe. Mr. Pfitzner asked Mr. Hotter to choose the songs by Mr. Loewe that he would sing, and Mr. Hotter chose some ballads that Mr. Pfitzner had orchestrated, thinking that his choices would please him. However, Mr. Pfitzner said to him after seeing a particular Loewe ballad he had selected ("Odin's Meeres-Ritt"), "Are you crazy? I am not [noted German pianist Wilhelm] Backhaus! I cannot play this!" Of course, Mr. Hotter immediately said that he need not sing that particular song, but Mr. Pfitzner said, "No. It's in the program. I asked you to choose [the ballads] and you have made this mess for me, and now I have to cope with it. See you tomorrow at 9 o'clock." Mr. Pfitzner worked both hard and quickly and the next day played the difficult passage in "Odin's Meeres-Ritt." Mr. Hotter said, "Fabulous!" Mr. Pfitzner replied, "Isn't it!" Mr. Hotter said much later, "He was so happy. He was in a better mood then than I ever saw him." Mr. Hotter was also impressed that such an accomplished composer had gone through so much trouble for a young singer. By the way, Mr.

Hotter once complained to Matthäus Roemer, his singing teacher, "What annoys me is that people say, 'Of course, it's so easy for you!'" Mr. Roemer replied, "You should take that as the highest praise. It is nobody's d*mn business to know how much effort it took you to sound so natural."[55]

• Sergei Rachmaninoff and Frances Alda are two famous names in music. One you would especially like to hear play the piano, and the other you would especially like to hear sing. Ms. Alda, a soprano, was playing piano at a get-together of musical notables when Mr. Rachmaninoff remarked to tenor John McCormack, "John, I want to play piano." Mr. McCormack picked up Ms. Alda and deposited her on a couch. She was going to protest, but seeing that Mr. Rachmaninoff was replacing her at the piano, she happily listened to him. By the way, Mr. Rachmaninoff and Mr. McCormack once listened together to a recording of Mr. McCormack singing "None But the Lonely Heart." Mr. Rachmaninoff said, "Is too slow." Mr. McCormack insisted that the tempo was correct. They argued for a while, and Mr. Rachmaninoff's wife finally went to him and whispered a few words of Russian. Mr. Rachmaninoff then told Mr. McCormack, "My wife tells me that you have a perfect right to your opinion — but you are *wrong*!"[56]

• Some music is created simply because the conditions are right. After the Harriott Quintet thought that they were finished recording one day, some of the musicians got ready to dismantle their equipment. However, Pat Smyth doodled at the piano, and Phil Seaman picked up his cowbell and hit it. It was pitched in A, and Mr. Smyth began playing in A. Shake Keane was having a drink, and he tapped the tumbler with a pencil — and the tumbler rang out with A. Coleridge Goode, the bassist, had a feeling that something good could come out of this, and he told the recording engineer, "Run the tape. Run the tape. We've got something here. We're going to play something." Joe Harriott came out of the control box, and everyone started playing, and the result was "Modal," a slow and pretty piece that appeared on the jazz album *Abstract*.[57]

• Many artists and musicians are concerned about money and about how many people are in the audience. Composer Sergei Rachmaninoff was one of these creative people. Conductor Walter Damrosch once asked Mr. Rachmaninoff what he was doing when he stared at the gallery. Mr. Rachmaninoff replied, "Counting the standees in the balcony. The manager told me they were not allowed, but there were forty-three." Mr. Damrosch's daughter Gretchen Finletter wrote that a manager "may grow nostalgic for the dreamy artist who does not understand about money, but he seldom has the pleasure of dealing with one."[58]

Conductors

• Arturo Toscanini played second cello in an orchestra that played the music of Giuseppe Verdi — with Verdi conducting it! While playing Verdi's opera *Otello*, Toscanini played the music as Verdi had written it, including a *pianissimo* in the last scene of Act 1. During intermission, Verdi came toward the cellists and asked, "Who plays the second cello?" Toscanini was so frightened that he could not move, so another cellist pushed him and said, "Ignoramus, when the great Verdi talks to you, stand up!" Toscanini stood up, and Verdi said to him, "Don't play too soft — play stronger." Toscanini objected, "Maestro, you marked *pianissimo*." Verdi replied, "Never mind. It must be heard — play *naturale*." From that experience, Toscanini concluded that a *pianissimo* in Italian music is different — louder — than a *pianissimo* in German music. Usually, of course, Toscanini closely followed the markings of composers. A famous conductor once led an orchestra in Robert Schumann's Second Symphony and then asked Toscanini for his opinion. Toscanini replied, "It was bad — all too slow. Why don't you follow Schumann's markings?" The famous conductor replied, "The markings are wrong. No good. They're too fast." Toscanini shouted, "I'd rather be wrong and close to Schumann than right and close to you!"[59]

• Conductor Herbert von Karajan believed that a new conductor ought not to work with a first-rate orchestra. Instead, give the conductor a 10th-rate orchestra. The conductor will learn much by trying to make the 10th-rate orchestra play like a 6th-rate orchestra. Mr. Karajan never spoke loudly during a rehearsal, and often he spoke little. He explained, "If I don't raise my voice, they'll listen to what I say, and the less I speak, the more important each word is." He could be critical. At the Lucerne Festival in Switzerland, he conducted an orchestra with an inferior bassoon player. Mr. Karajan had boated on a lake, and he had heard the sound of an alphorn carrying across the water from a great distance — a sound that Walter Legg, an English classical music producer, called magical. During a rehearsal, Mr. Karajan said, "Last night I heard an alphorn for the first time. Is there anybody here who plays it?" The inferior bassoon player pompously announced that playing it was mandatory in the Swiss schools. Mr. Karajan replied, "Pity it's not the bassoon."[60]

• Even a very talented conductor can make mistakes. Hans von Bülow once became upset at the beginning of a rehearsal of Brahms' "Tragic Overture" and called to the orchestra librarian, "Where is the contrabassoon? Why is there no contrabassoon engaged?" The orchestra librarian protested that no one had ordered that he engage a contrabassoon. Mr. von Bülow thought a moment, stopped being angry, and proceeded with the rehearsal. After the rehearsal, Mr. von Bülow gave the orchestra librarian $5 and said, "Do not say anything; it was my mistake. There is no contrabassoon in the Brahms Overture."[61]

• Conductor Sir Thomas Beecham and soprano Frieda Hempel may not have liked each other. Before singing in a performance of *Zauberflöte*, Ms. Hempel sent someone to Sir Thomas' dressing room to request that — since she was indisposed — he would transpose her aria. Sir Thomas agreed, but instead of making the aria easier to sing by transposing it down, he made it harder to sing by transposing it up.[62]

• Maestro Arturo Toscanini became terribly angry at tenor Leo Slezak because he swallowed a quarter note during a performance. Mr. Slezak begged for forgiveness, which Maestro Toscanini eventually gave. This forgiveness made Mr. Slezak, a large man, so happy that he picked up Toscanini, a small man, and kissed him on both cheeks. This enraged Toscanini more than before, and he stayed enraged at Mr. Slezak for two weeks.[63]

• The BBC once interviewed conductor Pierre Monteux and pointed out that conductors can be described in various ways; for example, one conductor can be described as a technician, another as a classicist, a third as a romanticist, and so on. The interviewer then asked how Mr. Monteux would describe himself. Given permission to describe himself in two words, not one, Mr. Monteux replied that he was a "d[*]mned professional."[64]

• While on tour with the Cleveland Symphony, violinist Josef Gingold was playing Tchaikovsky's Fourth Symphony — which frequently appeared on programs during the tour. Conductor George Szell leaned toward him after the first movement to ask, "Joe, take it easy. What are you giving so much for?" Mr. Gingold said, "George, I love this piece." Mr. Szell replied, "I love it, too. But not every night."[65]

• Conductor Arturo Toscanini and soprano Helen Traubel once had a disagreement about how a phrase should be sung. Maestro Toscanini decided, "We will try it my way and try it your way." After hearing both ways the phrase could be sung, Maestro Toscanini thought for a moment, then told Ms. Traubel, "Your way is better — we will do it your way."[66]

• Conductor Jeffrey Tate and his companion Klaus Kuhlemann keep in their home a collection of very valuable early Meissen porcelain, each piece of which cannot be replaced because of its rarity. According to Mr. Kuhlemann, "Our cleaning lady is terrified."[67]

• Like many conductors, Leopold Stokowski conducted without a score. This led to a misunderstanding, as a woman once said, "Isn't it a shame that the wonderful Mr. Stokowski can't read a score? Imagine how great he would have been if he only knew how!"[68]

Critics

• Nickelback has its fans; Nickelback also has its non-fans, including Josh Gross, who writes for the *Boise Weekly* in Idaho. When Nickelback came to the Idaho Center to play a concert, this is what Mr. Gross wrote: "You can spend $45 to go see Nickelback this week. Or you could buy 45 hammers from the dollar store, hang them from the ceiling at eye level and spend an evening banging the demons out of your dome. That $45 would also buy you a lot of pickles, which have more fans on Facebook than the band. It would also buy you an introduction to rock guitar video course that would allow you to surpass the band's skill level in five hours or less. $45 is also enough to see *Men in Black III* five times, buy a dozen Big Macs, do 10 loads of laundry or so many other experiences as banal and meaningless as seeing Nickelback but that come without having to actually hear Nickelback. But if you must, the band is playing the Idaho Center on Wednesday, June 13, [2012,] at 6 p.m. Tickets start at $45." (For what it's worth, the author of this book likes Nickelback.)[69]

• David L. Ulin is a critic for the *Los Angeles Times* (California). When he was in high school, he was a fan of Neil Young — he still is. One day, he was playing one of Mr. Young's albums — loudly — in his bedroom. His mother came to his bedroom and told him to turn down the volume. Mr. Ulin wrote much later, "When I protested that Young was a genius, my mother looked at me as if I were speaking a language she didn't understand. 'If he was a genius,' she told me, 'he wouldn't be playing electric guitar.'" By the way, Mr. Young undertakes what seems to be constant renovation, and he seemingly always eventually breaks up with whatever band he's playing in. In the middle of a tour with Stephen Stills in 1976, he sent Mr. Stills this telegram: "Funny how some things that start spontaneously end that way. Eat a peach. Neil."[70]

• Lotte Lehmann once sang the role of Elsa in *Lohengrin* and later learned that conductor Bruno Walter had been in the audience to listen to a new singer. She saw him the following day and waited for a few words about her performance, but he said nothing. Finally, she asked him if her performance had been so bad that he could say nothing about it. He replied, "Yes! Yesterday I saw something which I don't want to ever see in you, which doesn't go with you at all — routine." She listened to him. Later, she said, "Never again did I sing Elsa with routine." Like Mr. Walter, Ms. Lehmann believed, "Whatever we do or however often we do it, it must be each time reborn — each time a new creation. It is only when we are able to do this that we deserve the title Artist."[71]

• Men used to be shaved by barbers, who used a straight-edged razor to do the job because today's safety razors had not been invented back then. Of course, an accident with a straight-edged razor could be painful and bloody. Gioachino Rossini's barber once played first clarinet in one of Mr. Rossini's early operas. Mr. Rossini could be very severe with musicians who made mistakes during rehearsals, but even though his barber made many mistakes during rehearsals, Mr. Rossini never criticized him. By the way, Mr. Rossini used crosses to mark errors in his students' compositions. One pupil was happy that few crosses were marked in his composition, but Mr. Rossini explained, "If I had marked all the errors in the music with crosses, your score would be a cemetery."[72]

• A critic once criticized the German diction of operatic soprano Marilyn Horne. She telephoned the critic and started talking to him in German. The critic protested, "I don't speak German." She said, "This is Marilyn Horne, and I do!" Another kind of undeserved criticism occurred when Ms. Horne gave many recitals in places such as high school auditoriums. At one school, the only place she could go in between sections of the recital was the girls' bathroom, so she would go there to drink some water or wipe her brow. Her accompanist, Gwen Koldolsky, overheard a girl say to her mother, "I like that lady's singing, but why does she always have to go to the bathroom?"[73]

• Like many people in the arts, conductor Marin Alsop reads at least some of her reviews. Like many people in the arts, she tends not to remember the good reviews, but she definitely remembers the bad reviews. For example, she remembers her very first review, which she received after conducting a major concert in New York. The review stated, "We should think that this person is talented, but we don't." She says, "I stayed in bed for a couple of days after that."[74]

• In 1975, Beverly Sills made her Metropolitan Opera debut in *The Siege of Corinth*, which also starred Shirley Verrett and Justino Diaz. This production was much anticipated, and Ms. Sills wondered aloud during a rehearsal whether the critics would think the production had lived up to the anticipation. In those days of political correctness, Mr. Diaz said, "How can we miss? I'm a Puerto Rican, Shirley is black, and you're a Jew. Who would *dare* to criticize us?"[75]

• Herbert Hughes, the music critic for the *Daily Telegraph* in London, compiled a book of Irish melodies. At the request of tenor John McCormack, Mr. Hughes was his accompanist at a concert at the Hippodrome in which Mr. McCormack sang a number of those Irish melodies. Mr. Hughes was quite nervous, and after the concert, he said, "John, I'll never write another unkind word about an accompanist!"[76]

• After George Bernard Shaw heard a young Jascha Heifetz play the violin, he sent him this note: "Young man — Such perfection annoys the gods. You should play one or two wrong notes after each performance to appease them."[77]

Death

• Chick Webb was a jazz and swing bandleader and drummer, and he was a Good Samaritan. As a child, he suffered from tuberculosis of the spine and he became hunchbacked as a result. When a member of his band developed tuberculosis, Chick paid his hospital bills. He hired good musicians, and other bandleaders sometimes offered them more money and so they occasionally left his band. Trumpeter Taft Jordan said, "If a sideman left him, even without notice, Chick would take him back whenever the guy needed work." Chick once gave his vocalist Ella Fitzgerald a ring. She said, "I thought it was something he wanted me to try on for size for his wife, but he said it was for me." When Chick met Ella, she was orphaned and did not have a legal guardian, so Chick and his wife adopted her and hired her to sing in his band. He died of pneumonia on 16 June 1939. He said his last words to his mother, whom he smiled at: "Sorry. I gotta go."[78]

• Austrian conductor Karl Böhm disliked serving in the military as a young man because the officers were so autocratic. On a hot day during which he and his fellow soldiers had been drilling hard, he asked for a drink of water. The Lieutenant ordered him, "Back straight, knees bend, and hop to the fountain." Mr. Böhm obeyed the order, hopping approximately 300 meters to the fountain, but just before he reached it, the Lieutenant ordered, "About turn." Mr. Böhm then had to hop back to the other soldiers without having had a drink of water. Many officers were like that, and Mr. Böhm had little respect for what little intelligence they had. About one officer, he said, "I bet he'd sign his own death warrant." Mr. Böhm then filled out a death warrant for the officer, slipped it into a pile of papers that the officer had to sign — and the officer signed his own death warrant (which was not carried out, of course).[79]

• In 1974, music maven Quincy Jones suffered two brain aneurysms that could have killed him. Hospital staff shaved his head so that he could be operated on, and doctors estimated that he had a one percent chance of surviving the operation. In fact, the hospital staff kept his hair in case his family wanted it glued onto his corpse for an open-casket funeral. When he woke up after the operation, he discovered that family and friends had planned an elaborate memorial service for him, so he decided to go ahead with it. After all, his friend Frank Sinatra had once advised him, "Q, live each day like it's your last. And one day you'll be right." Mr. Jones attended his own memorial service with two metal plates in his head, and when he saw all of the talent that had showed up for the service, he thought, "That's some lineup."[80]

• Movie critic Roger Ebert's life may have been saved because he liked a long song by Leonard Cohen. He underwent surgery for cancer, the operation was a success, and he was scheduled to leave the hospital. Lots of hospital staff were present to wish him well, and for them he played on his iPod the song "I'm Your Man" by Leonard Cohen. While the song was playing, Roger's carotid artery ruptured. Of course, if your carotid artery must rupture, the very best place for it to rupture is in a hospital room where people who have the skills to save your life are surrounding you. Roger says, "If I'd forgotten the Leonard Cohen song, Chaz [Mrs. Ebert] sometimes reflects, we would have already been on Lake Shore Drive, and I would surely have bled to death."[81]

• Death is not optional: 1) Frederic Chopin was born at Zelazowa, Poland, on 22 February 1810, and he died in Paris, France, on 17 October 1849. At his funeral, earth from Poland was sprinkled over his grave. He had brought that earth with him from Poland 19 years previously. 2) Robert Schumann once visited the graves of Ludwig van Beethoven and Franz Peter Schubert, which are side by side in Vienna, Austria. He found a rusty steel pen on the top of Beethoven's grave and decided that Schubert must have dropped it there — Schubert died one year after Beethoven. Schumann used that pen to write his *B Flat Symphony*.[82]

• Organizers for the London 2012 Olympics contacted Bill Curbishley, manager of the Who, hoping to get Keith Moon and other members of the Who back together to perform at the opening ceremony. Unfortunately, Mr. Moon had died in 1978 from a drug overdose. Mr. Curbishley said, "I emailed back saying Keith now resides in Golders Green crematorium, having lived up to the Who's anthemic line 'I hope I die before I get old.' If they have a round table, some glasses and candles, we might contact him." In a blog post, *Guardian* journalist Brian Braiker joked, "For its part, the staff of the *Guardian* is just really looking forward to seeing Jesse Owens compete."[83]

Eccentrics

• Hasil "Haze" Adkins was a wild man of rockabilly and friends with Billy Miller and Miriam Linna of Norton Records. One thing they noted about him was he was a meat eater. Miriam says, "Hasil Adkins eats more meat than any other human being we've ever met; he carries Vienna sausages in his pocket." She once asked him, "What would you like for lunch?" He replied, "Meat." "Any special kind?" "Meat." One of Miriam's celebrity encounters was with artist Andy Warhol. She ordered him, "Stay right there!" Then she bought a can of Campbell's soup and made him autograph it. It was a prize possession for years, but she had to leave the house one day when Hasil was staying at her house, and she told him, "Haze, I'm going out for a while; there's plenty of food in the fridge." When she got back, he told her that he had eaten a can of soup. Billy says, "You guessed it —." Billy remembers that once a noisy ceiling fan bothered Haze in a club while he was playing, so he pulled out a gun and shot the ceiling fan so it did not interfere with his songs. By the way, in addition to marketing records by Haze, Norton Records also marketed records by Jack Starr, who did such things as making monster movies at home in addition to recording music. He also made his own Jack Starr Cologne — he once sent Norton Records a demo tape doused with the cologne, and Billy said, "I had to put it out on the window sill for about four days." As you expect, Miriam and Billy collect records. Miriam once was talking about her record collection with her eye doctor, whom she had known for 10 years. He told her, "I used to play in a band on Long Island called the Bell Notes; we recorded this 45 called 'I've Had It!'" Miriam says, "They were a band we had been looking for *high and low* [...] I was astounded. So now, whenever I see people who are like 40-plus, I feel like asking, 'Hey, did you ever make a record?'"[84]

• As you may expect, cartoonist R. Crumb was an eccentric when he was young. At ages 17 and 18, he wore a stovepipe hat that he had found in a junk store, and he wore a frock coat of the kind that Abraham Lincoln might have worn. He says, "I was a teenage social outcast. At the time it made me feel very depressed, and rejected by girls. Later I realized I was actually quite lucky because it freed me. I was free to develop and explore on my own all these byways of the culture that, if you're accepted, you just don't do. I was free to explore the things that interested me." One of the things that interested him was old-time music such as the blues. At age 17, he read a book titled *Jazzmen*, which included a Chapter about collecting old 78 rpm records. The author had collected many records by going to black neighborhoods, and so R. Crumb tried that. He would buy an old 78 record for a dime. He says, "That's how I discovered the old blues. It was unknown to me, it sounded very strange at first, but at the same time there was something very attractive about it, the way it grabbed you and got in under your skin, with cadence, with rhythm."[85]

• Jello Biafra, lead singer of the Dead Kennedys, collects really strange music. One kind of recordings that he likes is Do-It-Yourself Recordings. On one record that he has, you can hear the wife of one of the musicians say on the record, "Oh, are you recording? Should I turn the dryer off?" He has a DIY album that is rare because most copies were shrink-wrapped on a meat-packing machine — which melted most of the vinyl copies. By the way, Jello enjoys telling a story about German singer Heino, who wore sunglasses and a remarkable blonde hairdo on most of his album covers. A German band called Die Totenhosen — a punk band with humor — had a friend come onstage dressed as Heino with sunglasses and a blonde wig. He claimed to be the real Heino, and he and the band deliberately played Heino's songs very, very badly. This did not please the real Heino, and he sued. Apparently, he did not think that he ought to be the subject of parody. Die Totenhosen responded by having their fans attend the trial dressed like Heino.[86]

Education

• Naomi Yang of Damon and Naomi (with Damon Krukowski) fame learned to play bass basically on her own, after taking a few lessons from a teacher who knew his stuff but did not appreciate what he knew. The teacher gave her one lesson, and then he asked her to bring in some bass lines that she liked so he could teach her how to play them. She brought in the Joy Division song "Atmosphere," on which Peter Hook played bass, and the teacher told her, "He's playing a fifth, and then sliding up one octave." This is a simple move, and the teacher made the mistake of saying, "What a genius, huh?" This horrified Ms. Yang, who says, "That teacher had just handed me a miracle! That was one of the most beautiful and elegant things I'd ever heard, and it was so simple. Peter Hook wasn't doing something magical that I couldn't do; he was doing something very simple that I learned in Bass Lesson Number Two." But because the teacher did not appreciate the beautiful and elegant playing, she also thought, "I don't need this teacher anymore!" Still, he had taught her something important: "You don't have to be a virtuoso to play bass. You can play incredibly simple themes, but they can still be melodic and from the heart."[87]

• Ana Samways writes an entertaining humor column titled *Sideswipe* for the *New Zealand Herald*. Mike Hickey, one of her readers, sent in this anecdote, which Ms. Samways published under the title "Makes Simon Cowell seem sweet": "I was competing in a school holiday competition for singing, dancing musicians in a Waikato town hall in the 1950s when I received the ultimate put-down. I was in the third division in which there were only two entrants. Everyone was seated towards the back of the hall with the competitors marshalled in the front rows as they waited to compete. I had to sing first of the two in my division and when I finished there was a pause in proceedings. Then, to my horror, one of the judges came on stage and inquired, 'Who is the other singer in this division?' Another boy raised his hand. I was more than a bit demoralised when the judge said, 'We declare you the winner' and, looking towards me, 'because you couldn't be any worse than him!' He won without having to open his mouth!" This anecdote illustrates the truth that Humor = Embarrassment + Time.[88]

• The young Leonard Bernstein studied how to be a conductor under Fritz Reiner at the Curtis Institute of Music in Philadelphia, Pennsylvania. His father, Sam, gave him $40 a month to pay expenses — this was not enough money. Fortunately, conductor Dimitri Mitropoulos did the very good deed of sending Leonard a check for $225. Leonard did study hard, and Maestro Reiner respected him, but Leonard once made a mistake and called Maestro Reiner "Fritz" in class. Maestro Reiner responded — frostily — "Yes, Mr. Bernstein?" Maestro Reiner was known for having a temper. About him it was said, "Any day on which he failed to lose his temper was a day in which he was actually too sick to conduct." By the way, Leonard often missed classes while he was a student at Harvard, where he went to school before attending Curtis. On the top of a page of class notes, he once wrote, "hollow empty stupid dull uninteresting."[89]

• One of opera singer Clara Doria's teachers when she was young was Ignaz Moscheles, who had some definite ideas about playing the piano. Whenever a student had a finger improperly placed, he would catch the finger as if he were catching a fly. He also disliked the wearing of rings while playing the piano. Whenever a student wore a ring during a lesson, he would remove the ring and deliver a lecture on why piano players ought not to wear rings. The result, of course, was that his young students would borrow as many rings as they could so that they could wear them during lessons. Another very human trait he had was that he liked his own compositions. He once told his students, "Why do you spend your time in studying this meretricious modern stuff? You should confine yourselves to Bach, Haendel, Haydn, Mozart, Beethoven, Mendelssohn, and Me."[90]

• One of the things that David Amram learned from fellow musician Miles Davis is that jazz has no wrong notes. Mr. Ashram explains, "By that he did not mean to play anything — he had the most beautiful selection of notes imaginable. But he meant anything that you have can move to something else if you have a right path." For example, early in Mr. Amram's career he was playing French horn with Charlie Mingus, and the cash register went off while he was playing and it bothered him. Mr. Mingus said, "Next time that happens, play off the cash register. Use that as part of the music. If you're playing, the piano player is going blockity-block, the drum is going buckita-bucka-ding. Put that into the music and answer it. Go bita-boo-boo-bum and answer the cash register. Make that part of the whole experience."[91]

• While still in school, Elvis Presley was occasionally bullied, although he did have friends. When he was in the 8th grade while living in Tupelo, Mississippi, some bullies cut the strings of his guitar. However, his friends pooled their money and bought him new guitar strings. He and his family moved to Tennessee, where he attended Humes High School. He wore his hair long, which was unusual for males at the time, and when he tried out for the football team, some conforming bullies ganged up on him in the locker room, held him down, and were going to cut his hair. He was rescued by football star Red West, who became a lifelong friend. (A few days later, the football coach kicked Elvis off the team because Elvis declined to cut his hair.)[92]

• World-renowned concert pianist Byron Janis is also a teacher of music. He once had a gifted student, but she lacked artistry, and he needed to find a way to free her. By chance, one day he asked her if she always walked the same way when she went home after a lesson. She replied, "Yes." Mr. Janis then advised her to try different routes when she walked home: "You'll make new discoveries. It will be fun." The results were excellent. Mr. Janis says, "Within a month, I heard signs of the artist emerging. That simple suggestion seemed to touch the right nerve and her playing started showing signs of freedom. I was amazed. Strange — teachers never can predict what works."[93]

• Steve Baker taught English and drama from 1997 to 2002 to Alex Turner, who became the lead singer of the Arctic Monkeys. After Mr. Baker discovered that Alex had a band, he went to the band's website and wrote, "Well done, lads. I always thought you'd do something creative." Mr. Turner wrote back, beginning his message with "Hello, sir." Mr. Baker says, "Six weeks later, Alex got voted Coolest Man on the Planet by the *NME* [*New Musical Express*, a magazine about music], so ever since, I've started all my training sessions with the words, 'The coolest man on the planet calls me sir.'"[94]

• At age 84, the jazz saxophonist and flutist James Moody was still learning, the necessity of which he had learned early in his career and life. Part of the learning comes from practice, and part comes from books and advice. About practice, he says, "People would be improvising and I'd say, 'Boy, how did they know to do that?' Well, they practiced it.'" About other forms of learning, he remembers, "One day when I was with the Dizzy Gillespie Quintet, I looked at Dizzy and I said, 'Diz, I wish I would have studied music.' He looked at me and said, 'Moody, you ain't dead.'"[95]

• Conductor Pierre Monteux taught at a school for conductors, where a student conducted the prelude from *Tristan and Isolde* with very little feeling. Mr. Monteux stopped the romantic music and asked the student, "Tell me, young man, were you ever on the Grand Canal in Venice, on a beautiful moonlight night, with a beautiful young lady, with a beautiful décolleté, lying in your arms?" The student replied, "No," and Mr. Monteux said, "Too bad! Continue!"[96]

• Enrico Caruso once took up the flute. After he had taken a few lessons, a man asked him to play into the horn of a phonograph, and he made a recording of Mr. Caruso and then played the recording for him. Mr. Caruso asked, "Is that how I sound?" The man replied, "Yes. Can I sell you the record?" Mr. Caruso replied, "No. But I'll sell you the flute."[97]

Fame

• Fame can be a big negative. Courtney Love wrote the song "Teenage Whore" for her *Pretty on the Inside* album. The song contained the line "I'd give good money not to be ignored," but she soon started singing live the line "I'd give good money just to be ignored." Ms. Love sometimes has done things that cause her not to be ignored. Someone once said to her, "I remember you. You were on that plane ride from San Francisco to LA, and you were giving pills out to everyone with cool hair!" Ms. Love admits, "I couldn't remember it, but I knew it was true." She pursued Nirvana's Kurt Cobain, whom she eventually married, through the press. Whenever she did an interview, she asked if the interviewer was interviewing Nirvana the following week. If the answer was yes, she would give the interviewer a message to pass along: "Will you tell that Kurt Cobain that I have a *huge* crush on him?" Of course, the interviewer would think that she was crazy — sometimes she would add, "And tell him that I'm pregnant ... and my Daddy's mad about it."[98]

• Flutist Donald Peck stopped by a bar, where he saw Leonard Bernstein and some of his friends. Obviously, other people had noticed him — and sent over drinks — because in front of him were 10 drinks. A friend of Mr. Peck was in Mr. Bernstein's group and offered to introduce him to Mr. Bernstein, but after speaking to Mr. Bernstein, the friend became embarrassed and then explained to Mr. Peck that Mr. Bernstein did not want the bar patrons to know his identity and therefore he could not be introduced to him. This amused Mr. Peck, who writes, "Now, really — did he think the customers in the bar had sent those ten drinks to him as a complete stranger?"[99]

• Scottish singer Paolo Nutini says, "It's surprising what you find out about yourself when you become famous." For example, when he was walking into a bar he heard a woman call his name, but he thought, "I'm not turning round." She called his name again, but he thought, "Nope, I'm going to keep walking." He then heard the woman say to a friend of hers, "It's not him anyway — he's not got that big an arse."[100]

Chapter 3: From Family to Language

Family

• Katy Perry's real name is Katie Hudson, but she changed her name to avoid confusion with Kate Hudson, who was nominated for a Best Supporting Actress Oscar for her role in *Almost Famous*. "Perry" is Katie's mother's maiden name. (Katy did record her first album, which was self-titled and categorized as Christian/gospel, using the name Katy Hudson.) The road to the top was difficult. Some record companies dropped her before her first non-Christian album, *One of the Boys*, hit record stores on 17 June 2008; of course, it was a hit. Among its singles were "Hot N Cold" and "I Kissed a Girl." Katie's parents are evangelical Christians, and they have always supported her career. In the music video for "Hot N Cold," they play the roles of Katie's character's parents. Even with a hit album, Katie had to work hard. She performed outside during the Warped Tour, and at a concert in Maryland the weather was so hot that her shoes melted on stage. By the way, when Katie was a little girl, she was not allowed to watch any television episodes of *The Smurfs*. When she got a job doing voice work for the 2011 movie titled *The Smurfs*, she called her mother and said, "Guess what, Mom — I'm Smurfette!"[101]

• When Frank and Gail Zappa got married, he did not give her a ring; instead, he bought her a ballpoint pen — one that cost ten cents and was inscribed "Congratulations from Mayor Lindsay" — and pinned it to her dress. As you may expect, Frank was the parent who named their children. When Gail was pregnant with their first child, she asked Frank what to name the baby. He replied, "You can name her Moon or Motorhead." When Moon Unit was in the 6th grade, a classmate asked her, "Why did your parents name you Moon?" She replied, "Why did yours name you Debbie?" Another child is known as Dweezil, which is also the pet name Frank gave to one of Gail's toes. Another child is named Ahmet, after an imaginary servant the

Zappas had when they lacked real servants. They used to snap their fingers and say, "Ahmet? Dishes. Coffee, please." (Ahmet's other name is Rodan, after the Japanese monster.) And Diva got her name because she screamed when she was an infant. You may not believe this, but some of the Zappa children wanted to change their names when they were young. Moon Unit wanted the name Beauty Heart, and Dweezil wanted the name Rick.[102]

• Stevie Wonder — "Superstition" and "I Just Called to Say I Love You" are among his many hits — is blind, and when he was small, his young brothers thought that he needed more light in order to see, so they set a fire in a trash can and nearly burned down the house. Stevie remembers, "I know it used to worry my mother, and I know she used to pray for me to have sight someday, and so finally I told her that I was happy being blind, and I thought it was a gift from God, and I think she felt better after that." Stevie's mother was Lula Mae Hardaway, and his name at birth was Stevland Hardaway Judkins. The story is he acquired the name Stevie Wonder when he was discovered as a young boy and someone said, "That kid's a wonder!" Mr. Wonder once appeared on a poster for M.A.D.D. (Mothers Against Drunk Driving). Under his photograph appeared these words: "Before I ride with a drunk, I'll drive myself."[103]

• Rufus Wainwright grew up in a musical household: His mother is Kate McGarrigle, and his father is Loudon Wainwright III. After he was born and his mother was taking him home from the hospital, she stopped by her studio. No crib was there, so she laid him in a guitar case. Because of experiences such as this, Rufus says that he had no choice but to be a musician. Even as a child, he sang. At parties, his mother would have him stand on a piano and sing "Over the Rainbow." Rufus says, "I became aware at a young age of the power to sober up drunk people with my voice." Of course, Rufus has sacrificed for his music. In an interview with Laura Barnett, he points out that he has sacrificed "Rufus Wainwright the hausfrau. After so many years of being in hotels and backstage areas, I'm horridly inept at cleaning up after myself."[104]

• When he was growing up, Garth Brooks' family used to have a weekly night they called "Funny Night." Members of the family would sing, do imitations of famous people, put on skits, or do something else to entertain. This worked out well for Garth, who became a very famous country music star. While accepting an award for being 1991's Country Music Association's Entertainer of the Year, as the first President George Bush and his wife, Barbara Bush, were in the audience watching, Garth said that two famous Georges — George Strait and George Jones — were his inspiration, then he added, "No offense, Mr. President."[105]

• Joan Oliver Goldsmith is a volunteer singer in a chorus. Her father had taught her, "When bored in the symphony, watch the timpani," and so when she did not have to look at the conductor, she watched the percussionists. Once, she asked a member of the percussion department of the Minnesota Orchestra, "Isn't it awfully stressful? I mean, if the cymbals come in at the wrong place, everybody knows." He replied, "Yeah, but what are they going to do? Shoot you?"[106]

Fans

• Matt Groening, who is most famous for his long-running series of panel cartoons *Life in Hell* and for TV's *Simpsons*, is a music lover. As a young man, he loved some kinds of music that drove other people away. He says, "If my friends and I could drive people from the room when we put a record on, that was great." Another favorite activity was attending punk concerts, sitting in the balcony, and watching the audience: "To this day, there's nothing funnier than watching people being outraged by being bumped into while everybody else is slamming." For a while, he worked as a music journalist. He would recommend albums that no one would buy, and eventually he started making up band names and reviewing non-existent albums. One of the band names he invented was Chatterbox Punch Gruffy.[107]

• When author Wilborn Hampton was a young person, he and some kids from the neighborhood played Elvis Presley's new RCA record "Heartbreak Hotel" in a backyard. He and the neighborhood kids danced to the music. Suddenly, a neighbor lady opened her door and yelled, "Jezebels! You should all be ashamed of yourselves! That music is evil!" Then she went back inside. Wilborn and the others turned down the volume of the music a little and kept dancing. Certainly, people — especially females — reacted to Elvis strongly. Very early in Elvis' career, Mae Axton, a publicist for Colonel Thomas A. Parker, asked a girl who had been jumping up and down and squealing while Elvis sang, "Honey, what is it about this kid?" The girl replied, "He's just a great big beautiful hunk of forbidden fruit."[108]

• Joey Ramones, lead singer of the Ramones, was very likeable. In Japan, he went backstage at a Bob Dylan concert, and at that time people obeyed a backstage rule that stated, "Don't even look at him." Supposedly, people were required to stay away from Mr. Dylan and definitely not make eye contact. Best was simply to go into a room and shut the door if you saw Mr. Dylan coming down the backstage hallway. However, when Mr. Dylan saw Joey, he walked over to him and said, "Hey, Joey, my kids love your music."[109]

• Small things can make a fan happy. Jazz enthusiast and photographer Duncan Schiedt was once in a Fifty-Second Coffee Shop in New York when Sidney Bechet, who played clarinet and soprano saxophone in jazz groups, sat beside him, listened to the jukebox, and asked, "What's the name of that tune they're playing?" Mr. Schiedt answered, "Dill Pickles." Many years later, Mr. Schiedt says that "etched in my mind is the small pride I carried away from the event!"[110]

• All copies of the December 1989 issue of *Sassy*, a magazine for North American teenage girls, contained a flexidisc of R.E.M. covering the song "Dark Globe" by Syd Barrett. *Sassy* editor Jane Pratt walked by Tower Records and was happy to see that every copy of *Sassy* had been sold — until she noticed a trashcan filled with copies of *Sassy*. R.E.M. fans had bought *Sassy*, thrown away the magazine, and kept the flexidisc.[111]

• YouTube allows viewers to press a button to indicate whether they like or dislike a video. For example, when a video of the excellent A Touch of Class pop song "I'm in Heaven (When You Kiss Me)" was given over 1,500 likes and 24 dislikes. ATC fan Gemgurllove has a very plausible explanation for the 24 dislikes. She commented, "24 people were [so] busy pressing the replay button they pressed the wrong button!"[112]

Fathers

• Wynton Marsalis wanted to make his living as a musician, but many, many people advised him not to try. They told him, "Don't major in music because it's too difficult to make a living. You need a 'real' profession to fall back on when the dream dies." Fortunately for music lovers, Wynton followed the advice of his father, a man who knew firsthand how hard it is to make a living as a musician. Wynton writes that his father is "a great musician whom I had seen killing himself to make barely enough to take care of his family." So what is his father's advice? His father said, "Make sure you don't have anything to fall back on ... because you will. This is not for the faint of heart."[113]

• As of September 2013, Tori Amos had sold 12 million copies of her 13 albums. Her father was a pastor in Maryland, and when she was 13 years old, he knew that she would benefit from getting experience as a live performer of music. One day, he told her to dress in such a way that she looked older than she was, and then he took her to some bars in Georgetown in Washington, D.C. to look for a place that would allow her to perform. Tori remembers, "Mr. Henry's, a gay bar, gave me my first opportunity. My dad got flak from some parishioners, but he told them, 'I can't think of a safer place for a 13-year-old girl than a gay bar.'"[114]

• Walter Damrosch came from a musical family. His father was the famous conductor Leopold Damrosch. Walter once met in Germany a Royal Highness who was the niece of Emperor William. She knew about his father and asked him if he were "the son of the great Doctor Damrosch." Walter replied that yes, he was. She asked, "He played the viola, did he not?" Walter replied, "No, your Royal Highness, the violin." She said, "No, the viola." Walter wrote in his autobiography, *My Musical Life*, "This taught me that royalty must never be contradicted, even if they know 'facts' about your own father of which you are not aware."[115]

• When Roseanne Cash was 18 years old, she started to learn to play the guitar and sing country music. Her father, Johnny, heard her and sat down and wrote a list of "100 Essential Country Songs," including songs by Woody Guthrie, Jimmy Rodgers, the Carter family, Hank Williams, and Carl Perkins. He gave her the list and told her that to be a completely educated country musician she needed to learn those songs.[116]

• Not everyone likes modern classical music. As a teenager, caricaturist Sam Norkin was playing Jean Sibelius' First Symphony when his father demanded to know how the record player got broken. After that experience, Mr. Norkin played Sibelius only in the basement.[117]

Food

• Iggy Pop is an open interviewee. In a 1997 interview, he talked about his diet, which he does not regard as especially healthy: "I eat steak, I like a lot of butter on my toast, I like a lot of eggs, and I fart constantly, all day." However, Iggy does practice chi kung, which are Chinese exercises. By the way, his chi kung teacher is in many ways a regular guy. In the same interview, Iggy said, "It's funny because everyone expects him to be a vegetarian and very holy, but he's not. He liked to get f**ked and eat steaks, and he likes money — a lot. He's a guy, you know. He can also kill you in 800 different ways, but he'd rather just take your money legally. He's like that."[118]

• Southern Culture on the Skids (aka SCOTS) is a band that often asks audience members to come on stage and dance for fried chicken. The genesis of this came when the owner of a club they were playing in gave them a bucket of fried chicken. The chicken was on the side of the stage as they played, and a homeless man came into the club, saw the fried chicken, and started eating it. The band members told him, "Hey, that's our dinner, and if you want some of it, you at least have to get up here and dance with us." The audience loved this, and SCOTS kept it in the act. Bass player May Huff says, "It's good to feed a hungry crowd."[119]

• In August of 1975, five-year-old Debbie Gibson, future pop singer and writer of "Lost in Your Eyes," celebrated her birthday at her favorite restaurant — one that her family ate at twice a year: Christmas and Debbie's birthday. The restaurant allowed kids under age 12 to eat free, and Debbie ordered a very big, very expensive lobster, which she ate all by herself. She says that she looked a lot fatter walking out of the restaurant than she did walking in. She remembers, "Next time we went back, they had a special kids' menu. They wouldn't let little kids order from the big menu anymore — and that was because of me!"[120]

• Run-DMC performed all over the world, including Amsterdam, which has much more lenient drug laws than the United States. In an Amsterdam smoke shop, Jam Master Jay sampled the chocolate chip cookies, which were delicious, so he kept eating more and more of them, since he was not aware that they had a very special ingredient. When DMC noticed what Jay was eating, he told him, "Do you know what those are? Those are space cookies. Magic cookies. You're gonna be stoned for two days!"[121]

• Johannes Brahms enjoyed good food. One day, his doctor ordered him to stop eating rich food. The very next day, the doctor saw Mr. Brahms in a Viennese restaurant eating a feast of very rich food.

After listening to his doctor's criticisms, Mr. Brahms replied, "Do you suppose I'm going to starve to death just to be able to live a few more years?"[122]

• As a young woman traveling from town to town to make money by singing, Emma Abbott was often forced to eat less than she should. Once, she was so hungry that she sold her long hair in order to get money to buy food. Fortunately, she was discovered by opera singer Clara Louise Kellogg, who helped make her rich and famous.[123]

Friends

• Friends can be a big help when help is needed. While Jimi Hendrix was in the United States Army and stationed at Fort Campbell, Kentucky, some of his fellow soldiers did not like him and even beat him up once. One of Jimi's friends from Seattle, Washington, where he had been born, was also stationed there: Raymond Ross, the heavyweight boxing champion for the 101st Airborne. Raymond hit a few heads, and Jimi's fellow soldiers decided not to beat Jimi up anymore. As a young musician in Nashville, Tennessee, Jimi sometimes could not afford to replace his guitar's strings when they broke. As Jimi was trying to play his guitar without an E string, Larry Lee, a Nashville bass guitarist, gave him an E string. They became friends. When Jimi decided to go to New York City, he lacked a coat; Larry gave him one. By the way, much later Jimi asked Larry to play rhythm guitar for him at Woodstock. Also by the way, an element of luck is involved in becoming a member of a famous rock group such as the Jimi Hendrix Experience. Noel Redding, a white man, became bass guitarist for the group in part because he was a guitarist who had never played bass guitar before and so would not be limited by preconceived ideas about how to play bass guitar — more importantly, Jimi chose him because he liked Noel's Afro hairdo. Mitch Mitchell and another man were competing for the drummer position — Mitch got it because he won a coin toss.[124]

• When he was a young man, Leonard Bernstein met a man named Adolph Green, who later became big on Broadway and in Hollywood. When they met, each quizzed the other on his knowledge of music. They quickly discovered that neither was a fake and both would admit when they did not know something. Lenny played a few bars of music, said that they were by Dmitry Shostakovich, and asked Adolph to name the piece. Adolph said that he could not name the piece. Actually, the piece was by Lenny himself. Adolph then requested Lenny to play the piece titled *Puck* by Debussy. Lenny replied that he did not know that piece. Actually, no such piece existed. After the musical quizzing was over, the two became close friends. Betty Comden, who collaborated with Adolph for six decades, was impressed by Lenny when she first met him. She went home and woke up her mother and told her, "Mom, I've met my first genius." Her mother replied, "That's nice, dear," and then she went back to sleep.[125]

• Kinky Friedman once was walking when a Cadillac pulled up beside him and fellow country musician Waylon Jennings told him, "Get in, Kink. Walkin' 's bad for your image." By the way, Mr. Friedman once asked Willie Nelson, "Who were the most unlikely, spiritually weird golf partners you've ever had?" Mr. Nelson told him about going to the Bahamas to get away from the world for a while. He went to a golf course and saw John Lennon and John Belushi and played golf with them. The meeting was entirely accidental. All three of them were there to get away from the world, and none of them knew that the others would be there.[126]

• Like many musicians, George Duke stood outside of clubs that he was too young to enter just so that he could listen to the music. Later he became friends with Stanley Clarke, and the two appeared on each other's jazz albums so often that eventually they stopped charging each other. Instead, Mr. Duke would say to Mr. Clarke, "Look, you play two songs on my record and I'll play two on yours."[127]

Games

• Opera singer Nellie Melba occasionally gambled at Monte Carlo. She once lost the money she had with her and asked a friend named Baron Hirsch for a loan of 1,000 francs, which he reluctantly gave her. The next day, she sent him a check to repay the loan. Two days later, she received a gift from him: a diamond brooch. With it came this note: "Dear Madame Melba, You are the first woman who has ever paid me back money which she had borrowed. I am so touched that I have taken the liberty of buying you the enclosed little brooch, which I hope you will accept as a token of my admiration." Ms. Melba once saw an old woman who kept betting on the number five. She ran out of money and asked someone for a loan to put on the number five, but before she received the money the wheel began to spin. What was the number the ball landed on? Five. And Ms. Melba once saw someone put some money on red and some money on black and said that for sure she would win. The ball landed on zero.[128]

• Four members of the Cab Calloway band — Milt Hinton, Paul Webster, Hilton Jefferson, and Tyree Glenn — used to play pinochle together. At those games they would use vulgar language. But when they started playing bridge, their language became more refined. Mr. Hinton still remembers Mr. Glenn asking, "Sugarloafs, why did you trump my ace?"[129]

Gifts

• Early in their career, the Spice Girls demanded — and got — attention. Sometimes, they roller-bladed — without an invitation — into the offices of music executives. They also crashed music-industry parties. Ashley Newton, an executive for Virgin Records, remembers, "I'll never forget the day they burst in here. They caused such a commotion, doing a mad routine in the office, all talking at once and being funny." The Spice Girls signed with Virgin Records and soon sold millions of records. After they signed with Virgin Records, the Spice Girls threw a party for all of their parents as a way of thanking them for being supportive in the days before they learned their art. And when the Spice Girls met to record "Love Thing," Geri "Ginger Spice" Halliwell, gave all of her fellow Spice Girls gold rings inscribed with the word "Spice."[130]

• Comedian Russell Brand became engaged to singer Katy Perry in January of 2010. How did this come about? Partly through an exchange of gifts. During an awards show, they met backstage and liked each other. Mr. Brand later gifted her with a love poem, and she gifted him with a photograph of her breasts.[131]

Good Deeds (and Bad)

• At a concert featuring hardcore group Black Flag, a bouncer unnecessarily roughed up a woman in the audience. Black Flag bassist Chuck Dukowski saw what was happening, did not like what he saw, and hit the bouncer's head with the end of his bass, resulting in the bouncer going to a hospital to get stitches. After the show, Black Flag's kick drum was missing, and a different bouncer said that to get the kick drum back they would have to go to the manager's office. The kick drum was there, and so was the manager — who felt safe because his bouncers were also there. The manager criticized the Black Flag members, calling them "f**kups," but they got the kick drum. They also learned that the club's owner had called other clubs that Black Flag was going to play at and told these clubs not to pay Black Flag because they were troublemakers. Unfortunately, at this club and at other clubs women are often not safe at music concerts. In 1984, during a Black Flag concert in Hamburg, Germany, three women in the audience had their tops torn off. Mr. Rollins gave his shirt to one of the women, but his shirt was also torn off her body. Mr. Rollins says, "So much for my good deed." And at a club in Los Angeles, Mr. Rollins noticed that the security guys were frisking everybody who came in. He says that "[t]he girls got searched extra carefully" because "the security guys [were] getting in a good feel when they could." One way in which Mr. Rollins — a big, muscular man — is sensitive is that when he notices that he is walking behind a lone woman, he will slow down and let her put some distance between him and her. He knows that often women are afraid that they will get attacked on the street. He also knows that they can be scared by his presence. He says, "I've had girls run into stores and wait until I pass before they come out." Unfortunately, women sometimes have good reason to be afraid of men.[132]

• When Count Basie put together his 15-piece Count Basie Orchestra, it took time for the band to jell. They were playing at the Grand Terrace in Chicago, and they were supposed to play a score that the ballroom provided. Unfortunately, many of the musicians in the band could not read music, and they were forced to fake it. Trumpet player Buck Clayton said, "We had to do the best we could, which was nothing. We abused that show every night we were there." Fortunately, bandleader, composer, and arranger Fletcher Henderson saw the show, realized the musicians were struggling, and helped them. He lent Count Basie his own arrangements for the show, and he helped coach the musicians on how to play his arrangements. Count Basie said, "He was the only bandleader in the business who ever went out of his way to help me. Without his help, we would have been lost." Of course, the band soon jelled and became famous, and Count Basie helped other musicians, including a young Quincy Jones, whom he had met when young Quincy snuck backstage at a show by carrying under his arm a music instrument case — which was empty. Years later, Count Basie tried some of Quincy's arrangements and liked them very much — and made popular records out of them. Of course, Count Basie learned a lot while making music in St. Louis, Missouri, where musicians played hours and hours, including hours and hours after the show ended. One song could last a very long time. Pianist Sammy Price remembered those long jam sessions: He played, and then he left for three hours. He said that when he returned, "They were playing the same song."[133]

• Country singer/songwriter Hank Williams could be very generous. One day he was in a car with guitarist Clent Holmes driving. The car was filled up with various items, including fishing poles, but when they saw a hitchhiking hobo, Mr. Williams told Mr. Holmes to stop the car. Mr. Williams told the hobo, "We're full up and can't you take you anywhere, my friend, but here's some money so you can buy some food." (Hank Williams fan and biographer Paul Hemphill wrote in *Lovesick Blues*, "The way he [Mr. Williams] spread the wealth when he had it, you can be sure he didn't just give the fellow a couple of dollar bills." By the way, Mr. Williams worked with Fred Rose when recording his music. Mr. Rose helped manage Mr. Williams' career and once went to Decca and several other labels trying to find the right record company for Mr. Williams. After Mr. Rose walked out of a Decca executive's office, the Decca executive telephoned Mr. Williams and tried to take Mr. Rose's place, saying, "What can Fred Rose do for you?" Mr. Williams was loyal and snapped, "He's got you calling me, ain't he?" before hanging up.[134]

• The Dutch band the Ex makes odd music. They chose their name because it could be easily written on walls, and they drew straws to determine which band member would play which instrument. In 1983, they made four 7-inch singles about a closed factory in the area where the band formed: the Amsterdam suburb of Wormer. The band does have a sense of humor: For a year, it ran a 7-inch singles club, but the last single they sent out was 12 inches, so it would not fit in the box that held the 7-inch singles. The band is also capable of doing good deeds: It toured Ethiopia, giving free concerts in places where hardly any musicians, including Ethiopian musicians, went. The band members took along amplifiers and generators, but they left them behind for Ethiopian musicians to use. In addition, they gave away many free cassette tapes. Guitarist Andy Moor says, "Everyone still uses cassettes there. We went back to pressing up cassettes, giving them out to taxi drivers all over the place. So at least they know what we sound like."[135]

• Music photographer Jim Marshall could be abrasive, but he had many, many friends. In 1983, Steve Goodman was playing with Johnny

Cash in Eugene, Oregon. Mr. Goodman, who is famous for writing the song "The City of New Orleans," a hit sung by Arlo Guthrie, was suffering from leukemia, had lost his hair, and knew that he had little time left to live. Mr. Marshall avoided photographing his friend because of his lack of hair, figuring that his friend would not want his photograph taken, but after the concert, Mr. Goodman said to him, "Hey, Jimmy, I know that you're not taking pictures of me because of the way I look, but it's OK, man. I'd like to be in your book someday." Mr. Marshall promised him that he would be in the book, and a photograph that Mr. Marshall took appears in his first major book, *Not Fade Away: The Rock & Roll Photography of Jim Marshall*. Mr. Marshall writes about Mr. Goodman, "He was one of the real good guys and a good friend."[136]

• Taylor Swift learned how to play a 12-string guitar in part because of a bad deed and a good deed — and because of her own desire and determination. Here she explains the bad deed: "I actually learned [to play guitar] on a 12-string because some guy told me that I would never be able to play it, that my fingers were too small. Anytime somebody tells me that I can't do something, I want to do it more." A good deed helped her learn how to play. She explains that a computer repairman at her house helped her get started: "In this magical twist of fate, the guy who my parents had hired to come fix my computer [taught me]. I'm doing my homework and he looks round and sees the guitar in the corner and he looks [at me] and says, 'Do you know how to play guitar?' I was like, 'Ah, no.' He said, 'Do you want me to teach you a few chords?' After that, I was relentless. I wanted to play all the time."[137]

• Pianist Van Cliburn, who did not smoke or drink, did many good deeds in his life, including many before he became wealthy. Once, when his life savings amounted to a little more than $1,000, he donated that money to help buy a much-needed piano for the church he attended in New York City. He also gave up a $500 engagement — when $500 was a small fortune to him — to perform for free at a church banquet.

After visiting Russia, he carried back to the United States a lilac bush that a Russian fan of Sergei Rachmaninoff had asked him to plant at the head of Rachmaninoff's grave in Kensico Cemetery, Valhalla, New York.[138]

• For many years, Doc Severinsen and his band provided the house music for *The Tonight Show with Johnny Carson*. Mr. Carson stood up for his band. On one show Ray Charles performed, and on air he yelled to the drummer of Doc's band, "Pick up the pace!" After the show was over, Mr. Carson went to Mr. Charles' dressing room and said, "Ray, there's a drummer in Doc's band who needs an apology." Mr. Charles, a man of class, agreed that he had behaved unprofessionally: He apologized to the entire band.[139]

• When opera singer Helen Traubel's aunt and uncle suffered severe financial losses, she used to put $10 on her uncle's dresser each day — unasked — so he wouldn't be embarrassed by asking her for money.[140]

Husbands and Wives

• When Barbara Brooks, wife of country singer Kix Brooks of Brooks and Dunn fame, fell from a horse, she ended up in a hospital. One of the things she noticed was that a different person would appear each time she had to give a blood sample. The head of the department eventually apologized to her for this. The workers in the department were taking turns drawing her blood because they wanted to see the wife of a famous country and western singer.[141]

• In the documentary *Too Tough to Die: A Tribute to Johnny Ramone*, Rob Zombie says that Johnny told him that he and his wife, Linda, were walking down a street in New York. Johnny was carrying groceries, but when he saw a fan, he said to his wife, "Linda, take the groceries. I can't have a fan see me carrying groceries." Linda said, "F**k you, John. Then leave them in the f**king street." Rob says, "John was all about cool."[142]

Illnesses and Injuries and Rehab

• Jazz drummer Buddy Rich was a personal friend of Johnny Carson. When Mr. Rich became severely ill and worried that he might not ever play the drums again, one of Ed McMahon's friends called Mr. McMahon and said, "Ed, I'm going to make a strange request. Buddy is as down as a man can be. Would you and Johnny consider coming down to visit him? And the sooner, the better." Ed told Johnny that Buddy was ill, and Johnny immediately thought of a way to cheer him up: He and Ed would visit him and do a sketch with Johnny portraying Carnak the Magnificent. Carnac, of course, was gifted at divining the answers to questions. He would say the answer, and then he would open a sealed envelope that contained the question. As Johnny wanted, the jokes were somewhat bawdy. One example: Carnac stated that the answer was, "Dry hump." The question was, "What does a camel do after a bath?" The laughter therapy worked: Buddy made an incredible recovery.[143]

• Dee Dee Ramone, bass player for the Ramones, was heavily into drug abuse for a lot of years. (He eventually died of a heroin overdose.) According to a Ramones roadie, Dee Dee would sometimes ask to do cocaine with the roadies. They would lay out five lines of cocaine, but Dee Dee would snort more than the one line laid out for him — he would snort all five lines, then say, "Oops! I slipped." Dee Dee owned a cat named Orlando at a time when he was smoking lots of marijuana. Eventually, the cat came into the possession of Ramones tour manager Monte A. Melnick, who said that the cat was so high from all of Dee Dee's marijuana smoke that it was bouncing off the walls for a month before it calmed down. Mr. Melnick says, "Orlando is the only cat I've met that has gone through rehab."[144]

• In 1907, opera singer Enrico Caruso needed to visit a doctor, but he did not want the media to find out about the visit, so he decided to visit the doctor incognito; therefore, Mr. Caruso used the name of his voice coach and accompanist, Richard Barthelemy. Following the examination, the doctor said, "All right, Mr. Caruso, I'll get you well." Surprised, Mr. Caruso asked, "You know me then, doctor?" The doctor smiled and replied, "Mr. Caruso, after years on the stage of the Metropolitan Opera, do you present yourself here and expect to pass incognito? Why did you give me the name of your friend instead of your own? Don't you know that doctors are held to professional secrecy?"[145]

• Russian conductor Vasily Safonov got very seasick while crossing the Atlantic. Violinist Fritz Kreisler's wife was on board, and she tried to comfort him by singing the Russian national anthem to him, but he begged her, "Please don't do that, or I shall have to get on my feet."[146]

Invective

• Arturo Toscanini occasionally burst into fits of great rage during rehearsals. One such fit occurred when he was rehearsing the NBC Symphony Orchestra in Beethoven's Ninth Symphony. The rehearsal went along normally until the scherzo, but Toscanini became furious and accused the celli of playing without life, without bite. He accused the celli of taking it easy and insulting both him and Beethoven. He broke his baton, he ripped his score to shreds, and he pushed the conductor's stand off the stage. Then he pulled out his watch and threw it to the floor, shattering the watch and sending its parts in many directions. He swore that he would never conduct such jack*sses again, and then he stomped off to his dressing room, shouting insults all the way. The next day at rehearsal — yes, he did show up — he showed the members of the orchestra a cheap watch that he had brought — it bore the inscription "For Rehearsals Only." The rehearsal went exceedingly well. Samuel Antek, a violinist in the NBC Symphony Orchestra, wrote, "Toscanini's rage, somehow, always achieved a musical purpose. Childish, petulant, unreasoning as it was, we somehow respected and admired his capacity to be so moved and aroused by his feeling for his work." Toscanini really did feel that strongly about music. In Atlanta, Georgia, during a tour, the NBC Symphony entered a huge auditorium that smelled of horses and their manure because a horse show had recently been held there. A boxing ring was in the center of the auditorium because of a prizefight that would be held that night. The NBC Symphony Orchestra would rehearse now, and then play the following night. One workman who was wearing a hat walked by Toscanini, who knocked off the hat and said, "*Ignorante*! Take off the hat! Is a church here!" The workman was dumbfounded, so Toscanini explained, "Where is music is a church!"[147]

• Italian is rich in invective, and conductor Arturo Toscanini made rich use of it when he wanted to criticize a musician or a singer. Once, he was heaping Italian invective upon a musician when he realized that the musician did not understand Italian and so did not understand what he was saying. Because his knowledge of English was limited, Mr. Toscanini was forced to tell the musician, "You bad, bad man."[148]

Language

• Leonard Bernstein and his family spoke a language that he helped to create with a childhood friend named Eddie Ryback. They named the language with an amalgamation of their names: Ryback plus Bernstein equals Rybernian. Nina, Mr. Bernstein's daughter, explains, "It's basically a way of mispronouncing things — Yiddish words as well as people who just talk funny." A London *Times* article explains that "I love you" becomes "Mu-la-du," and the appropriate response is "Mu-la-dumus" ("I love you more"). Sometimes, Mr. Bernstein would put on what his children considered to be airs, and they would tell him in Rybernian, "La-lutt" ("Shut up"). Nina says, "[T]hat would bring him right down to earth."[149]

• Jazz banjo player Eddie Condon was witty. He once remarked about the 1940s bebop musicians, "They flat their fifths; we drink ours." And he once said about French writers who criticized American jazz, "We don't tell them how to stomp on grapes...."[150]

• In the early 1970s, saxophonist Pat Patrick asked Thelonious Monk, "What's happening?" Mr. Monk replied, "Everything is happening all the time — every googleplexth of a second!"[151]

Chapter 4: From Letters to Prejudice

Letters

• Richard Barthelemy, the voice coach and accompanist of Enrico Caruso, was French, and the French have a reputation for having a certain regard for a good turn of praise. A high-society woman once sent opera singer Enrico Caruso a very nice gift, which pleased him. Mr. Caruso sent back a souvenir, and he asked Mr. Barthelemy to compose a nice letter to accompany the gift. Mr. Barthelemy did compose the letter, and soon afterward the high-society woman invited him to lunch and said to him, "I have a favor to ask you, for which I desire secrecy. I am going to have you read an extremely charming letter from Monsieur Caruso in which he begs me to accept the lovely souvenir here. I want to thank him, and I've thought of you for that. Would you do me the pleasure of composing an answer to his letter which would have a true French turn to it? I'll recopy it and send it to Monsieur Caruso." Mr. Barthelemy composed the letter.[152]

• Manuel de Falla, a Spanish composer of romantic music, took his time answering letters, which piled up. When he learned that the Basque Spanish painter Ignacio Zuloaga had died, he said, "What a pity! He died before I answered his letter which he sent me five years ago."[153]

• Before Emmylou Harris became a famous country singer, she wrote Pete Seeger and said that she wanted to be a folk singer but she was afraid that she had not suffered enough. Ms. Harris said, "He wrote back to say life would come back and hit me hard soon enough."[154]

Mishaps

• Mishaps occur on stages, including opera stages. At the opening-night performance of *Julius Caesar* at the Metropolitan Opera, Spiro Malas, who played the role of Ptolemeo, forgot the first two words of his next aria. He went offstage to look up the words, and his small band of soldiers also went offstage. These "soldiers' were extras whose orders were to simply follow Mr. Malas wherever he went. Beverly Sills and the singers in the opera were amused because these are the two words that Mr. Malas had forgotten: "Julius Caesar." Of course, on-stage mishaps also occurred to Ms. Sills. While playing Queen Elizabeth in Donizetti's *Roberto Devereux*, Ms. Sills at first wore a putty nose to make her nose bigger, but she sweated so much during each performance that the putty nose fell off by the end of Act II, so eventually she performed the role with her own nose. Due to an automobile accident when she was a teenager, Ms. Sills had two capped teeth. During a performance of *Anna Bolena*, the caps fell out. She recovered them and continued to sing, and during a break her makeup artist, Gigi Capobianco, used Duco cement to make sure that the caps stayed in place. Ms. Sills said, "The only problem was that the next day the dentist had to use a hammer and chisel to remove them so that he could replace them properly."[155]

• Alice Cooper frequently gets "killed" by zombies as part of his act. He also uses a lot of stage props — something that sometimes results in accidents. For example, he used to "hang" himself on stage — a wire kept him from actually breaking his neck in the noose. Alice remembers, "We'd made the thing ourselves, and used piano wire as the support cable. But what we didn't figure is that if we used it 300 times, the wire would eventually lose its strength. Then one night in London it snapped. Fortunately, I instinctively put my neck up and slipped right through the noose. I fell 6 feet, hit my jaw. Man, was I lucky!" A live prop was a boa constrictor that once suffered from onstage diarrhea — something that made his stage crew, who were onstage dressed as clowns, vomit. (After the concert, Johnny Rotten said, "Alice, that was the most magnificent thing I've ever seen in my entire life.") Alice also stabbed himself in the leg with a sword — accidentally. He remembers, "I looked down and thought, 'Well, it's already in there, so I might as well carry on.'" Alice realized the importance of stage props from his days as a high-school student: "One of my teachers had a guillotine, and if you were late, he'd put your head in it. I was late all the time."[156]

• Almost everyone is familiar with *This is Spinal Tap*, a 1984 mockumentary directed by Rob Reiner, but not everyone knows that sometimes a version of something that occurs in the movie happened in real life to real bands. For example, the fictional band Spinal Tap had an on-stage disaster with a prop that was designed to look like Stonehenge. The prop was supposed to be 18 feet high, but due to a mishap was actually only 18 inches high. In real life, the real band Black Sabbath had trouble with a Stonehenge prop. Black Sabbath ordered a 15-foot-high model of Stonehenge, but the company that built it made it 15 meters high. Band member Michael "Geezer" Butler said, "It was 45 feet high and it wouldn't fit on any stage anywhere, so we just had to leave it in the storage area. It cost a fortune to make, but there was not a building on earth that you could fit it into." By the way, in American slang "Geezer" means old man, but Mr. Butler is British, and when he was growing up, in British slang "geezer" meant a good man or a cool dude.[157]

• Gerald Moore, world-famous accompanist, used to wonder why some Patronesses of Music knew so little about music. Emerald, Lady Cunard once grabbed Ida Haendel's very valuable Stradivarius by its strings and held it up in the air — Mr. Moore compared it to grabbing a parcel by the strings. Emerald, Lady Cunard then demanded to know why it was so valuable. Mr. Moore also stated that in the same drawing room, the hostess asked Sir Thomas Beecham, who with his orchestra were performing at a large party, "Sir Thomas, when are you going to play that lovely piece of Delius that you were rehearsing this afternoon?" Sir Thomas replied, "We have just this very moment played it, my dear." Speaking of Sir Thomas, one of his friends visited him in his dressing room after a Covent Garden concert and complimented him on the playing of his orchestra but also said that the orchestra had drowned out the singing of the vocalists. Sir Thomas replied, "I know. I drowned them intentionally — in the public's interest."[158]

• Cerys Matthews was the lead singer of Catatonia and now records solo albums. One of her best friends is fellow Welsh singer Tom Jones, who gave her the best advice she has ever received — and followed: "Tom Jones told me not to drink before going on stage. You grow up with all these myths about rock 'n' roll behavior, even if the stars are on a rollercoaster to hell. His advice was so simple, but it really does work." She had her most embarrassing moment on stage in the days before Mr. Jones gave her this advice, when she fell over a monitor during a concert in Germany. She remembers, "I might have got away with it if I hadn't been mid-note." Ms. Matthews has thought about death, as all of us have, and she would like to be remembered "with a good sentence on a gravestone. I'm still working out what it would say. Gravestones are like Twitter — you need something short that will amuse people."[159]

• Rumors spring up in odd ways. Opera singer Nellie Melba had a friend named Mrs. Hwfa Williams, who had a magpie that she named Melba. Ms. Melba sometimes stayed at the house of her friend. At a party, Mrs. Williams said to her guests, "Poor Melba has been terribly sick. I think it is because she had been eating so many mice." Ms. Melba wrote in her autobiography, *Melodies and Memories*, "Quite seriously the tale was spread around London that owing to my ravenous appetite for mice, my health had been impaired and I had been forced to stop singing."[160]

• Country musician Kinky Friedman once saw Kris Kristofferson talking to a young groupie. Mr. Kristofferson looked up and asked, "Kinky?" Mr. Friedman and the young groupie replied at the same time, "Yes."[161]

• While singing in *Aida*, Robert Merrill felt the strap of his sandal break, so he kicked the sandal into the orchestra pit. Unfortunately, a too-helpful musician picked it up and threw it back to him.[162]

Money

• Tenor Enrico Caruso made thousands of dollars each time he sang in an opera, and he was a talented caricaturist. One day, he and his wife, Dorothy, were walking along a street when he saw one of his caricatures — it depicted President Woodrow Wilson — in a store window. The price was not listed, so she asked his wife to go inside and inquire how much it cost. She did and found out that the price was $75, a good amount of money at the time. The price pleased Mr. Caruso, who joked, "Ah! Better we stop singing and draw!" Each week Mr. Caruso sent one of his caricatures to an illustrated Italian weekly titled *La Follia* that was published in New York by Marziale Sisca, one of Mr. Caruso's close friends. Mr. Sisca offered a lot of money to Mr. Caruso for these caricatures, but Mr. Caruso turned down the money, saying, "You are my friend. From friends I take no money. My work is singing. For that I accept payment. My caricatures are for my own pleasure, to give pleasure to others. Them I draw for nothing." On a transatlantic liner, he once was busy drawing a caricature of himself when a fellow passenger — a stranger — asked what he was drawing. Mr. Caruso replied, "A caricature of Caruso." The stranger exclaimed, "But that's yourself!" Mr. Caruso joked, "No. You see, Caruso and I look almost exactly alike. All I have to do, when I want to draw Caruso, is to do a drawing of myself."[163]

• Henry Rollins, former lead singer of Black Flag, is a serious acquirer of and listener to new music. He says that whenever he visits Melbourne, Australia, he walks into Vicious Sloth Records, throws his wallet onto a counter, and yells, "There it is, you b*stards! Take it all!" According to Mr. Rollins, the owners smile and start figuring out what to name their new houseboat. (Mr. Rollins is a stand-up comedian, among many other things, so he may be exaggerating.) Mr. Rollins also spreads music around the world. He says, "In my journeys, I have left literally hundreds of gigabytes of music behind in young people's computers all over the world." He has left behind the music of the

Ramones in Iran, the music of the Stooges in Sri Lanka, and the music of Fugazi in Bhutan. Mr. Rollins says, "When it comes to music, I am in constant acquisition mode. To me, getting the word out on new music is as equally important as acquiring it. In addition to utilizing my weekly radio show on KCRW, I mention bands in interviews and other ways as well. I have an agenda. I am on a mission."[164]

• By 2010, Lady Gaga had made a lot of money. So what is the best thing that she spent money on? She says, "I bought my parents a car." The car was a black Rolls-Royce. Lady Gaga says, "My dad's very Italian, so I wanted to get him a real Godfather car." She had the car delivered on her parents' wedding anniversary. When she told her father, "Go outside," at first he declined to do that. Why? Lady Gaga explains, "He thought I'd got him a dancing gorillagram." The car was decorated with a huge bow and this message: "A car to last like a love like yours." Her parents at first thought that the car had been rented for them to ride around in for a day, but she told them that the car belonged to them. Her father shouted, "You're crazy!" And he cried. By the way, Lady Gaga believes that it is possible to protect your privacy against the paparazzi — if you have and are willing to spend the money to do so. For example, after a concert in Berlin, some paparazzi in cars wanted to follow her, but they were unable to do so. She had hired two burly men to stand in front of their cars until she had vanished.[165]

• Fanny Brice got into show business by accident. At age 13, she took her brother to an amateur show, but unfortunately, she had only two quarters and all the seats that cost a quarter had been taken. To get into the theater, she told the manager that she wanted to perform on stage — her plan was for her and her brother to watch part of the show, but to sneak out before her name was called for her to perform. However, her name was called earlier than she had expected, she was forced to go on stage, and she sang "When You Know You're Not Forgotten by the Girl You Can't Forget." Fanny was so good that she won the first-place prize of $5, and she decided to go into show business.[166]

• Comedian Jack Benny loved music. Once he had the chance to get violinist Isaac Stern on the 3 February 1946 episode of his radio program. Mr. Benny's show allowed him to pay $10,000 per episode to the guest stars. He had already booked Ronald and Benita Colman for $6,000. Mr. Stern's fee was $5,000, but Mr. Benny gladly paid $1,000 out of his own pocket to book him. Mr. Benny, whose comic persona was that of a miser, said, "I got my money's worth. During rehearsals, I made him play about twenty solos for me, just for me, in my dressing room. I pretended I wanted to choose the best short number for him to play on the program. It was wonderful."[167]

• Conductor Karl Böhm noticed that in the foyer of the National Theatre in Munich, Germany, the musicians used to spit whenever they passed the bust of former General Music Director Herman Zumpe. He asked why they did that, and a musician replied, "It's been passed on from generation to generation, this spitting." They explained that musicians who had previously served there had petitioned the King for a raise in salary; however, Zumpe had commented, "I am against the raise; it's better to hunt with hungry hounds!" Thereafter, musicians spat first in his presence and later in the presence of his bust.[168]

• Opera singer Clara Doria had a servant named Natalizia who found an interesting way of making extra money: She sold locks of Ms. Doria's hair. She collected hair from Ms. Doria's combs and cut and trimmed the locks and tied them with a narrow ribbon. She then put each lock of hair in an envelope — also stolen from Ms. Doria — which she sold to youthful male fans of Ms. Doria. Natalizia had quite a business until some friends of Ms. Doria caught her selling these love-locks.[169]

• Musician Vicki Randle was the only woman in a band, and one of the males in the band asked her to sew a button on his shirt. She explained to him that she had never learned how to sew buttons because she was a musician. This action by the male sounds bad, but when the males in the band learned that she was making less money than they were, all together the males demanded that the manager pay her more money — as much as the male musicians were individually making.[170]

Mothers

• Bobby Henderson started playing jazz piano professionally by accident. He was at a New York City club called Pod and Jerry's, and the club owner said to him, "Hello, son, can you play the piano?" The club owner then pointed to a man, and said, "That's Willie 'The Lion' Smith you see there. He's one of the greatest piano players playing. Well, Willie's made plenty of money, and Willie's going to move downtown to another spot. ... So, play a tune, kid." Bobby was nervous, but he played "I Got Rhythm," relaxed, and played much more. He got the job, and he showed up that night to play for real and for money. He earned $150 in tips — a lot of money at the time. After work, he went home to his mother's house, and he emptied his pockets of all the paper money — 20s, 10s, 5s, and 1s — that he had earned and put the money on the kitchen dresser. In the morning, his mother woke up, went into the kitchen, saw the money, and screamed. Bobby woke up, went into the kitchen, and said, "What's the matter, Mom? House on fire?" He then explained that the money was his tip money from the previous night — he had not stolen it — and he told her to buy some new dresses.[171]

• The Dire Straits had a hit in 1985 with their song "Money for Nothing," which includes a reference to rock stars getting "chicks for free." A woman named Sally wrote in to Ana Samways' always entertaining *New Zealand Herald* column *Sideswipe*, "When I was little and my sister and I were in the car with my mum on a long trip, we also belted out off-key to the Dire Straits hit 'Money for Nothing' and I asked mum why he'd get 'chicks for free'. Clearly wanting to avoid having to explain the wild ways of rock stars, she told us the lyric was 'chips for free' and that when a rock star goes into a fish and chip shop, they have to pay only for the fish!"[172]

Music Videos

• Some of the comments on YouTube about music videos are funny. For example, a video of the Divinyls' hit "I Touch Myself" had 477 likes and 8 dislikes in May 2011. A person who calls him- or herself "Tomdotp" commented, "The 8 people that dislike this song touch themselves a bit too much!" And a person who calls him- or herself "TwilfsMind" commented about the video, "It's not about masturbation. It's about looking into your soul and finding out who you really are [...] Just kidding it's about Masturbating."[173]

• When the Ramones made the music video for their song "Pet Sematary," they filmed it in Tarrytown, New York, at the Sleepy Hollow cemetery, which is famous as the setting of some Washington Irving short stories, including "Legend of Sleepy Hollow." Among the celebrities appearing in the video were Deborah Harry and Chris Stein of Blondie, Ramones producer and co-writer Daniel Rey, the Cycle Sluts from Hell, and their dogs: the Cycle Mutts from Hell.[174]

Names

• Dave Matthews did not name his band the Dave Matthews Band. Instead, shortly after the group formed, a manager of a club needed a name to put on posters advertising the show. Band horns expert Leroi Moore told the manager to simply put "Dave Matthews" on the posters, as that was enough to ensure an audience, but the manager decided to add "Band" at the end. Mr. Matthews himself jokes that he would like to rename the band as "The Band That Used To Be Called The Dave Matthews Band But Isn't Any More Because It Was Wrongly Named To Begin With." Of course, Mr. Matthews is the leader of the band, and band concerts are known not just for the music, but for "Davespeak," which occurs when Mr. Matthews speaks about whatever he wants to, whether it is his favorite TV show or boxer shorts. Speaking of music, the Dave Matthews Band, like the Grateful

Dead, encourages tape-trading. Fans are encouraged to tape the shows and swap tapes with other fans. The Dave Matthews Band has even allowed fans to plug their recording equipment directly into the band's soundboard. Early in their career, it was possible to get a spot on the board, but now they are so successful that getting a spot may be impossible. (Tape-trading is distinct from bootlegging; bootlegging is done for profit, while tape-trading is not.) Tape-trading helped the Dave Matthews Band gets fans even in places it had not performed in before. Band violinist Boyd Tinsley remembers, "We'd never been to Alabama before. We'd go to this place, and cars would be lined up down the road, and there'd be all these people going to this big club. We'd be sitting in our red van saying, "Oh, my God!" Tape-trading also helped the Dave Matthews Band get a recording contract with a major record label. An intern brought a tape to his boss at RCA Records, and the boss liked what he heard. The boss telephoned another RCA Records VIP in New York to tell him about the Dave Matthews Band. (Full disclosure: Actually, the VIP in New York, Peter Robinson, was already planning to see the Dave Matthews Band in concert that very night.)[175]

• Rapper Kanye Omari West's mother, Donda, looked through books of African names to find the perfect name for him. *Omari* is Swahili and means "wise one." *Kanye* is Ethiopian and means "the only one." Of course, "K.O." is a boxing term and means knockout. Donda said, "I knew he would be our only child, set apart, and special." Kanye showed originality as a child, painting objects the colors he wanted to paint them. For example, he painted bananas purple. His mother let him paint the way he pleased. She said, "Kanye always had a distinct perspective. He always had his own spin on things." She did punish him when he needed to be punished. When Kanye was a teenager, she caught him watching an X-rated video. She made him research the effect that watching such videos has on teenagers, and she made him a write a paper on his research. Kanye is known for his self-confidence, of course, and his self-confidence kept him from getting a record contract early in his career. Columbia Records executive Michael Mauldin was interested in signing Kanye to a record contract, but Kanye bragged during the meeting with him that he was more talented than rapper Jermaine Dupri. Kanye did not know that Jermaine Dupri was Mr. Mauldin's son; Mr. Mauldin decided not to sign Kanye to a record contract. Kanye has the ability to grow as a person. Early in his career, he discriminated against gays, but when he learned that one of his cousins was gay, he changed his attitude. Kanye said, "It was kind of a turning point when I was like, 'Yo, this is my cousin. I love him and I've been discriminating against gays.'"[176]

• Neil Gaiman named his daughter Holly after a famous transvestite: Holly Woodlawn, an Andy Warhol superstar whom Lou Reed celebrated in his song "Walk on the Wild Side." When Holly was 19 years old, Mr. Gaiman played the song for her. As the song began, she said, "You named me from this song, didn't you?" Mr. Gaiman replied, "Yup." She listened to it carefully, really hearing the words for the first time: "Shaved her legs and then he was a she." She asked, "He?" Mr. Gaiman replied, "That's right. You were named after a drag queen in a Lou Reed song." Holly grinned and said, "Oh, Dad. I do love you."[177]

• *Sassy*, a magazine for North American teenagers, once mentioned the deodorant Teen Spirit, which it liked, but about which the *Sassy* writer also wrote the phrase "gag on the name." Supposedly, Kathleen Hanna, lead singer for the riot grrrl band Bikini Kill, read *Sassy* and then spray-painted "Smells Like Teen Spirit" on a wall at Kurt Cobain's dwelling. Of course, "Smells Like Teen Spirit" became the lead song off *Nevermind*, an album by Kurt's band, Nirvana. Also, of course, Kurt married Courtney Love, and they were very much in love. Courtney once apologized to Kurt because she had a zit, and Kurt replied, "Zits are beauty marks."[178]

• Larry Parnes was an early British rock-star manager. He often discovered talent and gave the performers new, more exciting names. Often, the first name was homey, and the second name was dynamic: Vince Eager, Georgie Fame, Johnny Goode, Dickie Pride, and Marty Wilde. Of course, some names were better than others. Vince Eager complained about another name that Mr. Parnes had thought up after giving Mr. Eager his name: "Why couldn't Larry have christened *me* Billy Fury?"[179]

• Rap stars can be interesting people. Two examples: 1) When he was growing up, Jay "Jam Master Jay" Mizell wore shoelaces in his sneakers that matched the color of his clothing. Why did he stop wearing laces in his sneakers? He explains, "It took too long to put them in." 2) Rap star L.L. Cool J can't be accused of being humble. His initials "L.L." stand for "Ladies Love," so his full stage name is "Ladies Love Cool J."[180]

Originality

• Musician Mirah Zeitlyn spent time in the early '90s in Olympia, Washington. While she was at Evergreen State College, she organized her record collection according to gender. Why? She explains, "Sometimes I want to listen to this stuff that men make, and sometimes I want to listen to this stuff that women make." Olympia is one of the places where riot grrrl music — which was influenced by punk music and feminism — started. In 1981, Sharon Cheslow was a founding member of Chalk Circle, the first all-female punk group in Washington, D.C. At a concert featuring the Mo-dettes, an all-female punk band from London, she had asked singer Romana Carlier for advice. Ms. Cheslow says, "I'll never forget the music she gave me. She said, 'You can't deny the fact that you're a woman, but the most important thing is to focus on creating music.'" Creating music is the most important thing, but another important thing is being free to create the music. Ms. Cheslow says, "I wasn't interested in joining some other culture. I wanted to create my own culture. That's what punk had taught me, that I should be free to create as a girl." By the way, some of the riot grrrls were adored. One fan wrote in a riot grrrl zine titled *MTM*, "I am considering calling the man/boy/guy/male who gave it to me a god." The "it" was a lock of the hair of Kathleen Hanna, who became one of the musicians who founded Bikini Kill in Olympia in 1990.[181]

• Ken Nordine is most famous for a series of *Word Jazz* albums. As a creative person, he leads a life of wit and originality. When he was a boy, he was bothered because his minister would not get wet during baptisms because he wore thigh-high boots. Therefore, young Ken secretly made a hole in one of the boots. He remembers that at the next baptism he "could *see* the Christian anger arise in [the minister's] reddening face. He walked out with a big boot full of water, and when he got to his study, he released a small flood!" Sometimes, the people around Ken are the original ones. For example, a man once stripped to his shorts and then painted himself white in Ken's garden. Ken called 911 and told the police about the man. The police arrived, thinking that Ken might be kidding them, but they found the man's pants and a bucket and paintbrush that the man had used to paint himself white. They then took off after the man, first radioing the police station to say, "The guy who painted himself white is heading north, and we've got his pants." Ken says, "If I were to *think* of something like that, people would say, 'Man, you are really sick.'" By the way, Ken's wife is also original. She once held a party, and it took Ken two hours to realize what was unusual about the party: Every man whom she had invited was named John. (She also thought about having a "Mary" party.)[182]

• Moby, who is most famous for the theme to Matt Damon's Jason Bourne movies, is an original guy. In a 1997 interview, he spoke about a family of cockroaches living in his apartment and often standing on a clock. Because of his born-again Christian beliefs, he would not kill them. Moby takes his Christianity seriously, but it may not be the Christianity that the reader is familiar with. At first, in the 1980s, he was celibate and did not indulge in alcohol and drugs; however, he realized that Jesus was not an ascetic person; after all, "he swore, and he drank, and he ran around, and he screamed at people. He loved his friends and was a very human, passionate figure. So I rejected that weird asceticism after thinking about who Christ really was and realizing that I was forcing myself to be something that didn't feel natural." As you may expect, people regard Christianity in different ways. Moby was signing autographs at a Detroit rock festival when a woman said to him, "I think it's really cool that you're a Christian." But the man standing beside her said, "You're a Christian? That's f**ked up." Moby said in the interview, "I wanted to say to them, 'Look, I like both of you, but neither one of you probably understands what that word means.'"[183]

• The Ramones sometimes opened out on tour for the band White Zombie — something that embarrassed White Zombie member Sean Yseult because she felt that White Zombie should be opening for the Ramones. The Ramones were grateful to White Zombie for taking them out on tour with them. Joey Ramone would tell White Zombie, "You guys are so cool for taking us out." The Ramones would also say that few bands would ask them to go out on tour with them. Ms. Yseult would reply, "Well, there's a reason. People are probably too scared to ask one of the greatest bands on earth to open for them." By the way, the band Sonic Youth sometimes opened for the B*tth*le Surfers (the band did not use asterisks in its name). Despite selling many more records than the B*tth*le Surfers, Sonic Youth had a good reason for opening for them. When the B*tth*le Surfers played, things happened such as beer getting spilled and chaos being rampant and mass numbers of people getting rowdy. By the time the B*tth*le Surfers had finished their set, the stage was always a mess, and Sonic Youth avoided playing in the mess by opening for the B*tth*le Surfers.[184]

• Culturcide became underground punk legends by taking other people's records, singing their own lyrics over top of the real lyrics, and then releasing the records. One thing they did was to sing their own lyrics over top of "We Are the World," a Live Aid/Band Aid single on which many major stars such as Michael Jackson and Stevie Wonder sang. Culturcide's version was "They Aren't the World," and some of the lyrics were "There comes a time when rock stars beg for cash ... There are people dying/whooah, and they just noticed." "We Are the World" was a good single that made a lot of money to help hungry people, but "They Aren't the World" is major-league satire that drove the music industry crazy and gave a lot of work to lawyers.[185]

• Mickey McGowan, creator of the Unknown Museum, enjoys collecting odd records. Among them is an album titled *Music to be Murdered By*. As you may expect, the portly suspense movie director Alfred Hitchcock introduces each musical selection and tells jokes in his distinctive voice: "Why shouldn't I make a record? After all, my measurements are 33-45-78." About a record titled *Companion to TV*, Mickey says, "When I played [it], I discovered it was absolutely silent — there's no sound on the record! Whoever made this was pro-television and wanted to make sure that if you got the urge to play a record while watching TV, you couldn't possibly interrupt anything."[186]

Photography

• Milt Hinton is an African-American jazz musician who took many, many photographs of fellow jazz musicians, both black and white. Whenever he would print a photograph of one of his white friends and the photograph came out dark enough for someone to comment on it, he would say, "I can't help it — that's just the way I see everybody."[187]

• In 1958, *Esquire* magazine commissioned Art Kane to take a group photograph of many jazz musicians. He took it at 10 a.m. on the front steps of a house in Harlem. Jazz musicians almost always work at night, and some of the jazz musicians who were in the photograph stated that they had not previously realized that a single day contained two 10 o'clocks.[188]

• If you want a good photograph of a band, it helps if the members of the band are looking in your direction. Bass player Alex James of the Blur remembers that one female photographer tried to make the members of the band look in her direction by flashing her breasts at them.[189]

Politics

• In 1979, Jello Biafra, the lead singer of the Dead Kennedys, ran a satirical campaign for mayor of San Francisco, during which his platform included such planks as 1) making everyone who worked in the business section wear clown costumes during business hours, 2) hiring back 7,000 city employees who had been laid off and making their job panhandling in rich neighborhoods at a 50% commission, 3) making police officers run campaigns to be rehired in the neighborhoods they patrol (residents in those neighborhoods would cast votes) and 4) legalizing squatting in buildings that were vacant because of tax reasons. As is the case with satire, his humor had a point. For example, he says, "In San Francisco, land of the homeless, there are so many buildings left empty for tax write-off purposes — it's obscene."[190]

• After Dan White, a former police officer and city supervisor, murdered San Francisco Mayor George Moscone and city supervisor Harvey Milk, he used the Twinkie defense (he claimed that eating junk food had diminished his ability to use his reason) to get only a 5-year sentence as punishment for committing the two murders. Jello Biafra, lead singer of the Dead Kennedys, regarded this as outrageous, and when he ran for Mayor of San Francisco, he ran on a platform one of whose planks advocated the erection of many Dan White statues in San Francisco — along with concession stands where people could buy eggs and tomatoes to throw at the statues.[191]

Practical Jokes

• Canadian jazz pianist Oscar Peterson once played a practical joke on singer Ella Fitzgerald. She owned a fur coat that her manager, Norman Grantz, had given her that she was very proud of. In the days before ballpoint pens, Mr. Peterson bought a trick ink bottle that came with a fake inkblot. He then visited Ms. Fitzgerald in her dressing room and made sure that she saw him writing with his pen. She warned him to be careful with the pen and ink because her fur coat was in the dressing room, and he said that she had nothing to be worried about. But when she left, he put the fake inkblot on her fur coat and upended the trick ink bottle. He was pretending to cry when Ms. Fitzgerald returned to her dressing room. She was a kind person; instead of displaying attitude, she comforted him. Mr. Peterson said, "She was more concerned about me than the coat." He called her "such a sweet person." Of course, people respected her singing. After she appeared at the Hollywood Bowl in Los Angeles, California, in 1956, a spectator commented, "Ella Fitzgerald could sing the Van Nuys [California] telephone directory with a broken jaw and make it sound good — and that's a particularly dull telephone directory." Occasionally, however, a member of an audience would start acting up while Ms. Fitzgerald was singing — and she would add new lyrics to the song and give that audience member a warning. And if a technical problem occurred on stage, she would sing about it and let the technicians know what the problem was. How good was Ella? She won 13 Grammies (and a 14th for lifetime achievement), and for 18 years in a row *Down Beat* magazine named her "Top Female Vocal Jazz Singer."[192]

• Music critic Henry T. Finck and Steven J. Jecko were friends at Harvard, class of '76 — 1876. They were regarded as musical prodigies, something they encouraged with a practical joke. They told their classmates that they could name each of a string of whatever notes that the other played. Mr. Finck sat at the piano and played several notes. Mr. Jecko then named several notes, and Mr. Finck said, "Correct." Then they traded places. Mr. Jecko sat at the piano and played several notes. Mr. Finck then named several notes, and Mr. Jecko said, "Correct." However, in advance each of them had agreed to say "Correct" to whatever notes the other named.[193]

• For a while, country singer/songwriter Hank Williams had a bad habit of borrowing cigarettes, reaching into one of his band members' pockets and taking a cigarette whenever he felt like it. He got cured of that bad habit after one of his band members found a novelty store that sold exploding cigarettes. By the way, Mr. Williams would sometimes write lyrics when traveling in a car from one gig to another. Once, he asked, "What rhymes with 'street'?" Guitarist and close friend Don Helms answered, "Your smelly feet!"[194]

• At the Metropolitan Opera, tenor Leo Slezak had just finished performing in Christoph Willibald Gluck's *Armide*. He saw an old, distinguished gentleman standing nearby, so he pushed him onto the stage, pointed to him, then bowed. Afterward, reporters asked him whom the old gentleman had been, and Mr. Slezak told them that it had been Gluck himself. The reporters printed the story, not knowing that Gluck had died in 1787.[195]

• André Previn once conducted the Chicago Symphony Orchestra at a rehearsal during which he asked the musicians to play a Russian composition that they had not played before. After they had gone through it once, Mr. Previn said, "That was wonderful! I have never heard an orchestra play so perfectly the first time! Now, let's try it again, and this time I'd like to hear a few wrong notes!" The musicians had fun obliging him by playing many wrong notes! He laughed.[196]

• Tenor Enrico Caruso didn't mind playing a practical joke on stage once in a while. While singing "*Che gelida manina*" ("Your tiny hand is frozen") to Geraldine Ferrar in *La Boheme*, he slipped a piece of ice into her hand.[197]

Prejudice

• In 1972, Yale University invited many black musicians to its campus in order to raise money for an African-American music department. The invitees included Eubie Blake, Duke Ellington, Dizzy Gillespie, Charles Mingus, Max Roach, Noble Sissle, Willie "The Lion" Smith, and Mary Lou Williams. While Dizzy Gillespie was leading a sextet in a performance, someone called in a bomb threat. The other musicians moved outside to play, but Mr. Mingus declined to do that, saying, "Racism planted that bomb, but racism ain't strong enough to kill this music. If I'm going to die, I'm ready. But I'm going out playing 'Sophisticated Lady.'" Outside, Mr. Gillespie and other musicians played Duke Ellington's "Sophisticated Lady," but from inside the theater building, whose doors were open, Mr. Mingus played his bass.[198]

• Jerry Lee Lewis' mother once told him, "You and Elvis are pretty good, but you're no Chuck Berry." Chuck Berry, of course, was a duck-walking guitarist who put 15 songs on the R&B Top Ten chart. By making hits such as "Maybelline," "Johnny B. Goode," and "Roll Over Beethoven," Mr. Berry helped integrate the United States, which during the 1950s was segregated in many places. He and Fats Domino, best known perhaps for "Blueberry Hill," toured together in the 1950s. At first, a rope divided the blacks from the whites, but later the black music fans and the white music fans mixed. Mr. Berry said, "Salt and pepper all mixed together." He added that Fats and he used to look at the mixed audiences and say, "Well, look what's happening."[199]

• Neil Spencer, editor of *New Music Express* (*NME*) from 1978 to 1985, points out that for a long time, female vocalists and musicians were expected to be eye candy. That changed with punk music and Poly Styrene and the Slits. Suddenly, female vocalists and musicians were not playing that game. Mr. Spencer remembers about the Slits, "Guys would shout at them. 'You look ugly,' and they'd reply, 'We're not here to look nice for you.'"[200]

• During the Jim Crow days, Bobby Womack toured with Sam Cooke, who gave him some advice. Mr. Womack said, "Sam used to tell me, whenever you got some money, you go get yourself a good ring and a good watch. Why would I need that? And Sam would say, you might have to get outta town quickly, before you get paid, and you can always hock that ring and that watch."[201]

Chapter 5: From Problem-Solving to Work

Problem-Solving

• Soprano Lily Pons once was supposed to sing several performances in Mexico City, but she became ill due to the high altitude. Nevertheless, she completed the first performance. The people who had hired her knew that she was ill, and they were afraid that she would leave without performing again, and so they locked her trunks and possessions in the opera house! Ms. Pons' manager took action to get her property back so she could leave. Ms. Pons said, "My manager hid backstage until five o'clock in the morning. When the night watchman was in another part of the house, the manager packed up my things and carried two big trunks down a creaking staircase. He loaded them on a flower cart drawn by a donkey, and hid them in the cellar of a friend's house." As it turned out, her manager did not need to do this. Ms. Pons adjusted to the high altitude and felt much better and so was able to complete the other performances. During World War II, she gave performances to Allied troops. In Italy, she performed very close to the front lines, and some soldiers in the audience had just returned from the fighting — she could hear sounds of combat during her performance. She noticed one soldier sleeping during her concert and worried about her performance, telling herself, "You must be slipping. You can't hold your audience anymore." But then she realized that the soldiers needed their rest. She said, "If music is able to rest these tired men so that they can relax and fall asleep easily, I'm doing what I came across the ocean to do!" After realizing that, she no longer worried if an exhausted soldier fell asleep during her performance.[202]

• British pop star Victor Fox was very good with children. In the late 1960s, he brought together a number of children from different schools to form a large children's choir at a music festival that was not located in London. They sang the English national anthem, but Mr. Fox wanted the children to sing louder, so he asked them, "This is the Queen's song, isn't it?" The children agreed. Then he asked, "Where does the Queen live?" The children replied, "In London." Finally, he asked, "Will the Queen be able to hear this?" The children shouted, "NO!" And then they sang loudly for the queen. (Here's another interesting bit of problem-solving. Dick Katz was a jazz pianist who always stomped a foot while he was playing. This usually was not a problem, but it became a problem when he was recording. To stop the noise of the stomp, he would put a cushion on the floor — unless he was stomping his foot, he couldn't play.)[203]

• Sarah Caldwell produced many operas in and around Boston at many venues, including the Cousens Gymnasium at Tufts University in Medford, Massachusetts. At the dress rehearsal with famous soprano Beverly Sills, a track meet took place — the orchestra accompanied thundering footsteps! Ms. Sills had a new business card made up: "Beverly Sills, Star of Stage, Screen, and Track." Ms. Caldwell and Ms. Sills worked well together. When Ms. Caldwell telephoned Ms. Sills and asked to act and sing the lead in the opera *Lucia di Lammermore*, Ms. Sills was so excited that she immediately said, "Yes." But after hanging up the telephone, she remembered something and so she telephoned Ms. Caldwell and said that she couldn't perform in the opera because she was pregnant. Ms. Caldwell asked, "Weren't you pregnant ten minutes ago?" (All worked out well. The costumer let out the costumes, and Ms. Sills performed in the opera.)[204]

• Philippe Rameau helped create the opera *Hippolyte et Aricie*, which was first performed in Paris in 1733. Audiences loved it; critics did not. Sarah Caldwell wanted to produce the opera in 1966, and she wanted to find the orchestra parts, which she was sure existed in the Paris Opera, a large part of whose music was not catalogued. She and opera company business manager John Cunningham went to the Paris

Opera Library, where they were assured that the music they wanted did not exist. Because Ms. Caldwell was sure that the music existed and was there, Mr. Cunningham romanced with wine and flowers a single lady who worked at the library while Ms. Caldwell looked jealous. Mr. Cunningham got access to the stacks in the library (which were normally closed to members of the general public), and soon he found the music that he and Ms. Caldwell wanted.[205]

• Out lesbian musician Anna Egge grew up in North Dakota and New Mexico — quite a change in climate. She remembers North Dakota as "a really beautiful, vastly open space. There's nothing there, so you have so much space and time in a day…. Just a lot of sky and land, great sunsets. It was beautiful." North Dakota, of course, gets very cold during the winter. Fortunately, people know to be prepared. Ms. Egge remembers, "On the school bus, we had to have a bag that was kept under our assigned seats that had an extra snow suit, an extra set of shoes, a can opener and two cans of food in case we got stuck in a blizzard!"[206]

• Opera singer Hans Hotter made a number of movies early in his career. In June 1939, he received his first film offer. His first film test was with middle-aged actress Käthe Dorsch, and it was not a success. However, Ms. Dorsch spoke with the movie producer and convinced him to have Mr. Hotter test with a younger actress. This second test was a success. Of course, Ms. Dorsch and not the younger actress starred in the film, and when Ms. Dorsch had a scene with Mr. Hotter, with whom she became friends, she would whisper to him, "Sorry it's me again, but imagine I am the younger one!"[207]

• Henry Lewis was talented in more than one way. At a Catholic school, he played a recital, but he forgot the middle of a composition by George Frideric Handel. No problem. He improvised some music that sounded as if Handel could have written it, and he got through the recital. Henry's father wanted him to go out for the football team. Henry went out for the team, made it, and immediately quit. Henry said, "I wasn't interested, but I wanted to show him I could do it." Later, Mr. Henry Lewis became a noted conductor.[208]

• Even when she was a child and needed to be babysat, Lady Gaga enjoyed shocking people. She used to strip completely naked, hide, and then jump out of hiding and surprise her babysitter. Lady Gaga's parents called her "Loopy." Of course, Lady Gaga grew up and started performing in small venues in New York City. Audiences there can be hard to please. When one audience began to ignore her, Lady Gaga stripped down to her bra and panties and then sang. The audience stopped ignoring her.[209]

Punk

• Ian MacKaye, co-founder and owner of Dischord Records, and member of the punk groups Minor Threat, the Teen Idles, Embrace, Fugazi, and The Evens, remembers going to a Ramones concert in 1979 in Virginia. Lots of people showed up for the concert wearing torn jeans because the Ramones' "uniform" consisted of T-shirts, leather jackets, and torn jeans. Unfortunately, the Ramones fans discovered that the concert venue had a dress code: no torn jeans. The fans went to a nearby pharmacy, bought needles and thread, and then went to the parking lot and started sewing up the rips in their jeans. Mr. MacKaye is an interesting guy with a strong work ethic and common sense. At concerts, he used to become angry when people would do senseless things such as bust up bathrooms. On stage, he would tell the audience, "The toilet is our friend — it takes the sh*t away. So what the f**k is going on? Every show, you f**king idiots break the toilets. It doesn't make any sense." Punk has a lot of sub-genres, and Minor Threat inspired a movement known as straight-edge, in which people abstain from alcohol and illegal drugs. (Henry Rollins, former singer of Black Flag, abstains from alcohol and illegal drugs.) Mr. MacKaye is credited with inventing the term "straight-edge." Fans who were straight-edge would sometimes draw an X on both of their hands because bars would draw a symbol on patrons' hands to indicate that they were of legal age and could buy alcohol — the X's were a counter-symbol to the bar symbols. By the way, Mr. MacKaye says that he was not a good student while he was in high school. He disliked writing book reports, and almost always he would not read the book. When he had to write a book report on *One Flew Over the Cuckoo's Nest*, he ended up calling the home of the author, Ken Kesey. (Mr. MacKaye says, "I called 555-1212 and asked for Ken Kesey's number in Oregon.") Unfortunately, Mr. Kesey was out of town, but his wife talked to Mr. MacKaye for 45 minutes and relayed to him a number of Mr. Kesey's ideas. Mr. MacKaye says, "Not only did I immediately write a report and get an A on it, but I f**king read the book because I couldn't believe she had been so kind to me. [...] Kids are always calling me about sh*t. I'm always happy to talk to them."[210]

    • When punk came to Los Angeles, the bands needed a place to play. Because punk was so different — and sometimes violent — finding a place to play could be difficult. A man named Brendan Mullen got drunk and stumbled down some steps and found a place that resembled an underground cavern. For a while, punk bands played shows at the newly named Masque. But due to problems with things such as bringing the space up to city code, that did not last long. Another place they found to play in was a pseudo-Polynesian restaurant/bar owned by Madame Wong in Chinatown. A few shows were held there, but a show with the Bags turned into a disaster, with punk fans turning over tables and chairs. Madame Wong decided to keep on having punk shows there, but without punk bands such as the Bags that had female musicians. Apparently, she reasoned that the female musicians drive punk fans wild, causing them to be destructive. Fortunately, any band that was banned by Madame Wong was able to go to the Hong Kong Cafe and play. The bands that had been banned were able to enjoy revenge. Someone left a tape for Madame Wong, and when she played it on her sound system, a voice screamed that all real punks should go to the Hong Kong Cafe and hear some "real music."

The punks left. Another case of revenge occurred in San Francisco when someone kept a punk group called the Nuns from opening for Blondie, featuring Debbie Harry. The Nuns gave a free show at the same time Blondie was performing, reducing the number of fans at the Blondie concert. By the way, although hardcore punk bands can be frightening, often the punk musicians are dedicated to their music. Joe Dirt, the drummer for the F**k-Ups (a band that did not use asterisks in its name), wanted the group to put out a record, but the band had no contract with a record company and it had no money. Mr. Dirt got a job as a subject in a two-months'-long medical experiment and used the money he earned to fund the record.[211]

• In the late 1970s, the punk group Crass had a good response to people who would say, "That lot think the world owes them a living." In this day of big bank bailouts, big automobile company bailouts, and big business using its big money to move American jobs overseas, Crass' response to the DTOUAL question — Do They Owe Us A Living? — is very relevant: "OF COURSE THEY F**KING DO." Punk critic Steven Wells is very aware that music by Crass is basically unlistenable, but he respects their ideas and realizes that Crass was very influential. One thing that Crass did was to produce Do It Yourself records that included their own booklets that were filled with information about smashing the system that was trying to bring you down. A cartoon once showed a punk buying a Crass record, throwing the record away, then eagerly reading the booklet that came with the record. (Mr. Wells quotes a critic who described Crass' music as reminiscent of "two lathes buggering each other on an elevator in an aircraft hangar.")[212]

• C.J. Ramone (Christopher Joseph Ward) took over on bass after Dee Dee Ramone (Douglas Colvin) left the Ramones. As a youth, he started out playing the drums, but he says that he ran into a problem: "When I was young, I played drums, but they must have been too noisy because I came home one day and they were gone." Another Ramones drummer was Marky Ramone (Marc Bell), who says, "I've always drummed in their style — steady and hard-hitting — but it was difficult working myself up to the speed. There are three speeds in the Ramones: fast, pretty fast, and very fast." The Ramones' first album — which was self-titled — is regarded as one of the greatest and most influential rock albums ever, but some critics — of course — did not like it. Stephen Ford referred to their speed when he wrote in the *Detroit News*, "They don't waste their time — they waste yours."[213]

• Punk rockers and their predecessors have done many strange things. Iggy and the Stooges once put water in a blender, turned it on, put a microphone over it, and broadcast the sound for 15 minutes before beginning their normal set. Sid Vicious of the Sex Pistols looked the part of a punk rocker and had the image, but he could not play his bass guitar well — not even well enough to play punk music, which was famously amateurish. Steve Jones usually played the bass parts that appeared on recordings. During live shows, the Sex Pistols sometimes did not even turn on the amp for Mr. Vicious' bass.[214]

Recordings

• At the 2006 Mercury Music Prize (a British award) ceremony, Richard Hawley's 4th solo album, titled *Coles Corner*, was nominated but did not win. Instead, an album by a group called Arctic Monkeys — his friends — won. While accepting the award, Arctic Monkeys frontman Alex Turner said, "Call 999, Richard Hawley's been robbed." This remark was widely quoted, with the result that Mr. Hawley began to become famous. Mr. Hawley says, "It changed things for me. I started selling f**king records." In 2007, he recorded another album, *Lady's Bridge*, although his father died while he was recording it. Actually, his father gave him some advice that helped him finish recording the album. Mr. Hawley says, "One of the last things he said to me — apart from, 'Don't forget my f**king beer and fags [cigarettes] when you come tomorrow' — was, 'You'd better finish that bloody record. Don't get crippled by grief.'"[215]

• Live recordings were difficult to do in the days when recordings were made on wax cylinders because the microphones often picked up sounds that should not have been picked up. One live recording of a Cesar Franck symphony was ruined when near the end of the symphony, the wax cylinder recorded a woman saying quite loudly and clearly to another woman, "Tell me, dear, where do you buy your stockings?"[216]

• The music of a jukebox in a bar can get annoying after a while. That's why CBS in 1953 produced a record titled "Three Minutes of Silence," which gave exactly that when a customer selected it from the records in a jukebox.[217]

Rehearsals

• Conductor Arturo Toscanini desired excellence from the singers and musicians he worked with, and sometimes he vented his displeasure during rehearsals. This occasionally had the unfortunate effect of making singers and musicians nervous, resulting in more mistakes. In Salzburg, Austria, Lotte Lehmann sang Eva in *Die Meistersinger* for Maestro Toscanini, a conductor of genius. He was not satisfied during rehearsals, and at one rehearsal, Ms. Lehmann said that Maestro Toscanini "wrapped himself in an icy silence and just looked at us sadly and scornfully." Finally, Ms. Lehmann said to him, "Maestro, won't you please tell us what crime we have committed? We want to do everything you want, but won't you please tell us *what* you want?" Maestro Toscanini replied, "There is no fire!" Hearing that, Ms. Lehmann, the other singers, and the musicians decided to focus on the fire and not on avoiding mistakes. Ms. Lehmann thought to herself, and so apparently everyone else did, "Let us forget that it is the much-feared maestro before whom we are singing. Let us forget that we must be exact to the finest detail. Let us forget that any and every mistake is a deadly sin. Let us just be normal human beings, who are not without faults, like this genius — then the fire will blaze which had been dampened through our fear." The result was magical, and after the rehearsal, Ms. Lehmann went to Maestro Toscanini's dressing room. He was only scantily dressed, but she hugged him, said, "Thank you, Maestro," and left.[218]

• Leonard Bernstein was rehearsing *Falstaff* when the trombone choir failed to hit a note in unison. This surprised Maestro Bernstein, as it wasn't a hard note to hit in unison. Caricaturist Sam Norkin was watching rehearsal, and from his seat, he could tell what the problem was. The music stands of the trombonists did not contain the music of *Falstaff*; instead, they held such reading matter as the Racing Form, the *National Enquirer, Reader's Digest*, and the sports page from the New York *Daily News*.[219]

• Early in his career, Walter Midgley worked in a variety program. At the band rehearsal, he went to a lot of trouble to get some of the rough edges smoothed out among the musicians, but at the performance he noticed that the musicians seemed to have forgotten everything he had taught them earlier at the band rehearsal. Therefore, he spoke to the conductor, who told him, "Oh, that was a different band you were rehearsing with."[220]

Riot Grrrl

• Both punk and riot grrrl music believe in Do-It-Yourself (DIY) when it comes to creating music and other art. In 1994, a drunk and enthusiastic 16-year-old girl named Lauren Goften approached Rachel Holborow, who worked for the English record label Slampt. Lauren told Rachel about her riot grrrl band Kenickie, which she said she had formed with some schoolmates. Rachel was so intrigued by what she heard that she asked for a demo tape. Actually, the band existed only in Lauren's head. Also, Lauren and her schoolmate Marie du Santiago did not know how to play musical instruments. No problem. They learned how to play two chords and started writing songs and recorded their first tape: *Uglification*. They then learned to play a third chord and started playing in public. Lauren, whose band name was Lauren Laverne, remembers that she forgot how to play her guitar solo while on stage, so she sang it instead. Basically, the band learned how to play by playing on stage and they learned how to write songs by writing them. So what happened? Alan McGee, head of Creation Records, took a plane to see them. He liked what he heard and offered to sign them to a record deal. They turned him down. Kenickie was active from 1994 to 1998, recorded for Fierce Panda and EMI, and when they broke up, lots of female fans mourning the breakup sent letters for months to the music magazines *NME* (*New Musical Express*) *and Melody Maker*.[221]

• Frequently, the question "Stones or Beatles?" comes up in discussions about music. Someone asked that question to record producer Guy Picciotto. He replied, "The Smiths." Beth Ditto, lead singer of Gossip and a supporter of riot grrrl music, has two good answers to the question "Ramones or Sex Pistols?" One answer is this: "The Slits." Another answer is to ask this question in reply: "Heavens to Betsy or Bratmobile?"[222]

Songwriters

• Country songwriter Harlan Howard knew that the young Hal Ketchum was planning to come to Nashville, Tennessee, and so he invited him to stay at his house: "I know you're coming up. You're trying to get a publishing deal or a record deal. So just stay at my house." Staying at Mr. Howard's house had some major benefits, such as hearing people such as Mr. Howard, Waylon Jennings, Allen Reynolds, and Jim Rooney talk and play music. Mr. Howard told the young Mr. Ketchum, "Listen twice and talk once; maybe you'll learn something." Mr. Ketchum played a couple of songs that were clever rather than honest, and then he played a folk song titled "Someplace Far Away." Mr. Howard listened to the song and then told Mr. Ketchum, "That's it — that's where you need to go." He added, "One thing you need to bear in mind as a songwriter is that it's all been said before. If you can just learn to say it from your own perspective in some kind of honest fashion, people will gravitate toward it. [...] we're all telling the same story, but if you do it from your own heart and your own perspective, people will get it."[223]

• So where did the title of John Lee Hooker's song "Boom Boom" come from? He got the title from a bartender named Luilla at the Apex Bar in Detroit. Mr. Hooker was playing with a band, and he always arrived late. Whenever that happened, and it always happened, Luilla pointed at him and said, "Boom boom, you're late again." Mr. Hooker recognized a good song title when he heard it, so he created a song, and it was a hit first for him and later for the Animals. What about Luilla? Mr. Hooker says, "She went around telling everyone 'I got John Lee to write that song.' I gave her some bread for it, too, so she was pretty happy."[224]

• Steven Tyler of Aerosmith is a hard-working man. For a while, he and the band spent so much time on the road that even when he was home he would wake up and automatically telephone for room service. By the way, he wrote all the lyrics to the songs on the Aerosmith *ROCKS* album, but accidentally left them in a manila envelope in a taxi. Mr. Tyler says, "I lost the whole thing — all the words to the songs. I had to go back to the Ramada Inn on 8th Avenue and sit with the headphones and bring it all back. I got about 50 percent of it. Can you imagine what was in that cab that went into the wastebasket?"[225]

• Some people know what they want. Carole King met fellow songwriter Graham Nash and asked, "So when are we going to write together?" He replied, "I'm not the guy." She then said, "Oh, fine. I'll be at your house at one o'clock." He asked, "What?" She replied, "I'll be at your house at one o'clock and we'll write." He said, "Didn't I just get through telling you?" She replied, "I don't care what you just said. I'm coming to your house at one o'clock. We can do this." She came to his house at one o'clock, and they wrote a good song together.[226]

• Songwriter Steve Earle is not shy when it comes to expressing his opinions. Wearing his cowboy boots, he once stood on songwriter Bob Dylan's coffee table and proclaimed, "Townes Van Zandt is the best songwriter in the world." He later met Mr. Van Zandt, writer of "If I Needed You," who told him, "That's a really nice quote, but I've met Bob Dylan's bodyguards, and I don't think [what you did] is a really good idea."[227]

Television

• On 12 June 1936, Ella Fitzgerald recorded her first song, "Love and Kisses," which she made with the Chick Webb Orchestra. The record was in a jukebox at a nightclub, but Ella was not allowed in the nightclub because she was underage. She remembered, "So I had some fellow who was over 21 go in and put a nickel in while I stood outside and listened to my own voice coming out." The turning point in Ella's life came in 1934 on an amateur night at the Harlem Opera House in New York City. She and two friends drew straws to see who would perform on stage, and Ella drew the short straw. She had intended to dance, but performing immediately before her were two sisters who danced much better than she did, so instead of dancing, she sang "Judy," a song made famous by the Boswell Sisters. Ella was a hit with the audience and won $25. She called this "the hardest money I ever earned," but added, "Once up there [on stage], I felt the acceptance and love from the audience — I knew I wanted to sing before people the rest of my life." In her later years, Ella made a commercial for Memorex recording tapes. In the commercial, she hit a high note and broke a glass. Then a Memorex recording of Ella's high note was played, and it broke a glass. The commercial then asked, "Is it Ella, or is it Memorex?" A boy once attended one of Ella's concerts and afterward said, "I liked her singing all right, but she didn't break no glass."[228]

• While doing research for *The Drew Carey Show*, Mr. Carey and his producer, Bruce Helford, stopped at a local pub in Lakewood, Ohio, where they heard some musicians play "Moon Over Parma," a song that one of them, Bob "Mad Dog" McGuire, had written. The song is about a man who gives his girlfriend a bouquet of radishes. At best, Mr. McGuire thought that the song would be popular locally, so he was surprised when Mr. Carey and Mr. Helford said that they wanted to use as it the theme song to *The Drew Carey Show*. He ended up getting $750 to $1,000 each time the song opened the show. Mr. McGuire says, "It's kind of like having another job but not having to go to work."[229]

Travel

• World-famous accompanist Gerald Moore detests background music, of which he writes, "I find it difficult to indulge in the process of thinking even at the best of times, but when this slime is being poured into my ears, thought or study or reading are quite impossible." He once asked an American stewardess to turn off the background music during a flight. She did, but remarked, "Not musical, eh?" Of course, as an in-demand international accompanist, Mr. Moore frequently traveled. He once undertook a sea voyage to Dublin, Ireland, from Holyhead, Wales. He boarded in the evening, drank two large whiskeys, and slept soundly. The next morning, he told a steward, "That is the way to cross the Irish Sea. I slept undisturbed the whole night, unaware of any tossing and pitching, rock 'n' roll." The steward replied, "No, sir, you wouldn't have felt much movement. You see, we haven't cast off yet. It's been too rough."[230]

• According to Michael Sellers, the son of British comic Peter Sellers, Henry Mancini, the composer of "Moon River," liked to smoke weed, and he carried it with him when he traveled. Peter Sellers once asked him, "But what about Customs?" Mr. Mancini replied, "Who's going to bust the man who wrote 'Moon River'?"[231]

Work

• For a while, Michael Sembello, although he preferred jazz, played guitar for Stevie Wonder. A friend got Mr. Sembello to audition by pretending that they were going to a place to jam, but he did mention that Stevie Wonder would be present. When Mr. Sembello found out that it was an audition, he was ready to leave immediately. For one thing, about 200 people were there to audition, and the wait would be very long to play. His friend, however, waited until no one was looking and erased the first five names on the audition list and put his name and Mr. Sembello's name first. Mr. Wonder was going in a different, more jazzy direction at this time, and so Mr. Sembello had an advantage on the other guitarists although they knew the Stevie Wonder catalog of hits. Mr. Sembello remembered, "It was kind of like a game show for guitar players: if you hang in there you got to stay, but if you screw up you were eliminated." Mr. Sembello got to stay. At one point, Mr. Wonder played some songs from an album that had not yet been released, but Mr. Sembello "copped the changes immediately." When Mr. Wonder asked him how he was able to do that, Mr. Sembello replied that he had a good ear. Mr. Wonder asked if he had heard the new album, and Mr. Sembello replied that he had not. Mr. Wonder asked an assistant, "Is the album out yet?" No, it was not. Next question: "How the hell do you know these tunes?" "I don't know the tunes. I'm just guessing where you're gonna go." "You've got the gig." "I didn't come here for no gig — I just came here to jam." Mr. Sembello ended up taking the job. He said about the experience of working for Mr. Wonder, "I had all the technical ability in the world and could play like the fastest guitar player in the West, but he was the one who taught me the most about feel."[232]

• Arthur Whittemore and Jack Lowe became a two-piano team by accident. In 1935, when Arthur was 19 years old and Jack was 18 years old, Arthur's aunt invited him to visit her in Puerto Rico. Arthur wanted his friend Jack to come with him, so he told his aunt that he and Jack were a two-piano team and so Jack had to come, too, so they could continue to practice together. His aunt invited Jack to visit, and she arranged a two-piano concert for Arthur and Jack to play in San Juan, Puerto Rico. As soon as they found out that Arthur's aunt expected them to play a two-piano concert, the two young men immediately began to practice together. They had no music for two pianos, so they transcribed famous musical classics. The concert was so successful that they decided to continue working as a team. This is fortunate for music history because they were so good, and because both were so gregarious that they probably would not have worked as solo piano virtuoso pianists because they would have hated being lonely while traveling on tour. One of their prized possessions was a letter from twentieth-century French composer Francis Poulenc, to whom they had sent a copy of their recording of his *Concerto for Two Pianos and Orchestra* — the orchestra was the New York Philharmonic, conducted by Leonard Bernstein. Mr. Poulenc wrote, "Your performance of the *Concerto*, like that of [Vladimir] Horowitz of my *Toccata*, is the one for posterity."[233]

• Mariah Carey worked hard to become the major musical success she is. When she was a teenager, she got very little sleep. During the day, she worked in a restaurant, and at night she went to a music studio, writing and recording songs until 7 a.m. Then she slept for "a couple of hours," she says, and woke up and did the same thing again. Some of her older musician friends were amazed at what she was doing. They would ask her, "Why are you working so hard?" Ms. Carey says that she knew that they were "loafing about in the middle of the day," and she would think, "Because I don't want to be like you." Her first five singles all reached No. 1 in the United States. She has a bit of a reputation for being a diva, but she says, "I try not to be a jerk. I really do." She also says that rumors about her are just that: rumors. For example, she says, "They said I wouldn't come into a hotel unless there were petals on the floor. I'm like, do you really think at 3 a.m. I give a s**t what I'm walking on?"[234]

• Quite a number of hit records feature the work of studio musicians such as drummer Hal Blaine, who was inducted into the Rock and Rock Hall of Fame in 2000. Often, the studio musicians played all of the music while the stars simply sang. Mr. Blaine played drums on the recordings of the Beach Boys' "Wouldn't It Be Nice?," the Byrds' "Mr. Tambourine Man," the Carpenters' "(They Long to

Be) Close to You," the Mamas & the Papas' "Monday, Monday," Elvis Presley's "Can't Help Falling in Love," Simon and Garfunkel's "Mrs. Robinson" and "Bridge Over Troubled Water," and Frank Sinatra's "Strangers in the Night." Nowadays he listens to an oldies station, which has advantages and drawbacks. He says, "It's an amazing ego trip since I'm on so many of the songs. But it has its drawbacks. *You* hear your youth. *I* hear a day at the office or a divorce."[235]

• In 2006, Ben Knox-Miller and Jeff Prystowsky formed the music group Low Anthem. The two men had been friends and a late-night DJ team at the college radio station of Brown University in Providence, Rhode Island. Mr. Knox-Miller remembers "playing jazz records through the late-night shift: 2 a.m.-5.30 a.m. Those are the golden hours for radio. The only people who are listening at that time are crazy people who have psychoses that keep them up in the wee hours, calling in to us and saying some really creepy, strange stuff." And Mr. Prystowsky says, "They were so desperate for DJs at that hour. If you were willing to stay up, you got the job. We would exclusively play upright-bass jazz solos, for three and a half hours, non-stop. I saw it as our job to aid our listeners in sleeping, and, heck, everyone sleeps through a bass solo."[236]

• Musicians can be fired for odd reasons. Nicky Byrne of the boyband Westlife, which was started in 1998 by Louis Walsh, who had put Boyzone together, remembers that Mr. Walsh wanted the musicians who worked for him to be professional: "Louis always said he wanted hard workers rather than heart-throbs (or even talented singers)." Mr. Walsh twice fired all the members of Westlife. Mr. Byrne explains why: "He even sacked us twice for messing around; once, very early on, for throwing bread rolls at each other, while strolling in late for meetings. I remember him losing it, shouting: 'You've let it all go to your heads. I don't work with people like that.' Thankfully, he listened when we begged him to take us back."[237]

• Producer Steve "Mr. Mig" Migliore started small with a studio in a room in the home of a friend's parents in Philadelphia, Pennsylvania. He and the friend charged $25 an hour to produce and mix songs. But after a friendly music attorney named Brad Rubens introduced him to the major labels, he became big quickly. Mr. Migliore was broke and flipping hamburgers in a food court when he discovered that his remix of LeAnn Rimes' "How Do I Live" had reached the top spot on *Billboard*'s adult contemporary chart. He immediately said, "Does this mean that I have a career?"[238]

• Photographer Jim Marshall was using strobe lights as he took photographs of T-Bone Walker, and he asked Mr. Walker if he minded the lights. Mr. Walker replied that the lights did not bother him. He used to play music behind a wall of chicken wire so he and his fellow musicians wouldn't get hit with bottles and other debris. And one time a guy who had shot somebody came into the bar. The bar manager told them to keep playing, and they did until the shooter passed out and the police arrested him. So, Mr. Walker said, "[T]hem lights don't bother me none."[239]

• When Jerry Lee Lewis was still a teenager, he performed for $15 a night, playing from 1 a.m. until dawn at an after-hours bar run by Roy Hall on Commerce Street in Nashville, Tennessee. Jerry Lee was the youngest person there, and patrons let him hold onto their watches and jewelry because they figured that because he was so young, police would not search him if they busted the bar. Sure enough, police busted the bar, and Jerry Lee, who had at least 15 wristwatches on his arms, was the only person who was not searched.[240]

• Jazz guitarist Freddie Green worked for a long time with Count Basie, but Count Basie laid him off when during a period of financial difficulty he went from leading a big band to leading a small group that did not include a guitarist. However, Mr. Green did not want to be laid off. Therefore, he simply showed up for a gig — even though Count Basie had not called him to come back and work. Simply showing up to play had the desired result. Count Basie welcomed Mr. Green back and started giving him a paycheck again.[241]****

• Frank Churchill and Paul Smith wrote beautiful music for Walt Disney, and they won Academy Awards for their music. One day, Mr. Disney was showing some guests — Charlie Chaplain and H.G. Wells — around his studio, and they all walked into the room where Mr. Churchill and Mr. Smith were supposed to be writing the music for *Snow White*. Apparently, the two composers were taking a break from music; instead of composing music together, one composer was setting on fire the other composer's fart.[242]

• Krissi Murison was the first female editor of *NME* magazine, aka *New Music Express*. When she was 15 years old, she was into music in a big way, and put green dye in her hair and tried to play guitar and sing in a band. She certainly looked the part of an indie music chick, but she admits, "I had absolutely no musical talent. I played a bit of really bad guitar and I tried to sing. I was so bad at guitar that when we played gigs they would just turn my mic down so I would just look the part."[243]

• In 1960, jazz guitarist Jim Hall couldn't afford a telephone. Jazz tenor saxophonist Sonny Rollins was reclusive and didn't want or have a telephone. Nevertheless, they communicated. A note by Mr. Rollins appeared in Mr. Hall's mailbox one day. Mr. Hall then put his own note in Mr. Rollins' mailbox. They exchanged notes for a while, and when Mr. Rollins decided to start playing jazz in public again in 1961, he offered Mr. Hall a job playing in his pianoless quartet.[244]

• The early punk rock group Television wanted to play music at CBGB's, so they asked owner Hilly Kristal for permission. He asked what kind of music they played, and in return they asked what the sign "CBGB-OMFUG" meant. Hilly told them it meant "Country, Bluegrass, Blues, and Other Music for Uplifting Gourmandizers." The members of Television then lied and said that that was exactly the kind of music they played.[245]

• Chicago tenor saxophonist Von Freeman started playing professionally at age 12. When he showed up for his first day at work, he gave this note from his mother to the nightclub manager: "Don't let him drink, don't let him smoke, don't let him consort with those women, and make him stay in that dressing room." The nightclub manager told him to do something to make himself look older, so he drew a mustache on his face.[246]

• Harry "Sweets" Edison played jazz trumpet for Count Basie, but he almost quit shortly after being hired. The band played mostly without written music, and Sweets wasn't sure what notes to play. He told this to Count Basie, who knew that Sweets could play and who told him, "If you find a note tonight that sounds good, play the same d*mned note every night!"[247]

• Communism has some major faults, including giving way much power to petty bureaucrats. One city official insisted that musicians paid to perform in a park must play for eight straight hours with no intermissions. When the musicians protested, the official stated, "The Government knows best what is and is not possible."[248]

• For various reasons, people decide to make their living creating music. The Mississippi Sheiks' Walter Vinson, who used to work as a field hand, had a very good reason for quitting and taking off with his guitar to play country blues: "I'm not going to spend the rest of my life behind a mule that's farting."[249]

• Marian Anderson was a famous singer of opera and African-American spirituals. Occasionally, someone would tell her that they would do anything to be able to sing like her. She would smile and then ask, "Would you practice eight hours a day?"[250]

Appendix A: Book Bibliography

Aberback, Brian. *Black Sabbath: Pioneers of Heavy Metal*. Berkeley Heights, New Jersey: Enslow Publishers, Inc., 2011.

Adams, Joey. *The God Bit*. Boston, MA: G.K. Hall & Co., 1975.

Angel, Ann. *Janis Joplin: Rise Up Singing*. New York California: Amulet Books, 2010.

Anjou, Erik. *Dave Matthews Band*. Philadelphia, PA: Chelsea House Publishers, 2002.

Antek, Samuel. *This was Toscanini*. With Eighty-four Photographs by Robert Hupka. New York: The Vanguard Press, 1963.

Aretha, David. *Awesome African-American Rock and Soul Musicians*. Berkeley Heights, New Jersey: Enslow Publishers, Inc., 2013.

Balfour, Victoria. *Rock Wives*. New York: Beech Tree Books, 1986.

Barthelemy, Richard. *Memories of Caruso*. Trans. Constance S. Camner. Plainsboro, NJ: La Scala Autographs, 1979.

Belsito, Peter, and Bob Davis. *Hardcore California: A History of Punk and New Wave*. Berkeley, CA: Last Gasp of San Francisco, 1983.

Benny, Jack, and His Daughter Joan. *Sunday Nights at Seven: The Jack Benny Story*. New York: Warner Books, Inc., 1990.

Bessman, Jim. *Ramones: An American Band*. New York: St. Martin's Press, 1993.

Blackburn, Julia. *With Billie: A New Look at the Unforgettable Lady Day*. New York: Vintage Books, 2005.

Blum, David. *Quintet: Five Journeys Toward Musical Fulfillment*. Ithaca and London: Cornell University Press, 1999.

Böhm, Karl. *A Life Remembered: Memoirs*. Trans. John Kehoe. London and New York: M. Boyars, 1992.

Borge, Victor. *My Favorite Intervals*. London: The Woburn Press, 1971.

Bowe, Brian J. *The Ramones: American Punk Band*. Berkeley Heights, NJ: Enslow Publishers, Inc., 2011.

Brook, Donald. *Singers of Today*. Freeport, NY: Books for Libraries Press, 1971.

Brown, Anne K. *Katy Perry*. Detroit, Michigan: Lucent Books, 2011.

Burch, Gladys, and John Wolcott. *Famous Composers for Young People*. New York: Dodd, Mead & Company, 1939.

Burden, Zora von, editor. *Women of the Underground: Music*. San Francisco, CA: Manic D Press, 2010.

Caldwell, Sarah. *Challenges: A Memoir of My Life in Opera*. With Rebecca Matlock. Middleton, Connecticut: Wesleyan University Press, 2008.

Carpenter, Angelica Shirley, and Jean Shirley. *Robert Louis Stevenson: Finding Treasure Island*. Minneapolis, MN: Lerner Publications Company, 1997.

Carson, Mina, Tisa Lewis, and Susan M. Shaw. *Girls Rock! Fifty Years of Women Making Music*. Lexington, KY: University Press of Kentucky, 2004.

Couric, Katie. *The Best Advice I Ever Got: Lessons from Extraordinary Lives*. New York: Random House, 2011.

Damrosch, Walter. *My Musical Life*. New York: Charles Scribner's Sons, 1923.

Deffaw, Chip. *Jazz Veterans: A Portrait Gallery*. Photographs by Nancy Miller Elliott and John & Andreas Johnsen. Fort Bragg, CA: Cypress House Press, 1996.

Dessau, Bruce. *George Michael: The Making of a Superstar*. London, Sydney, and Auckland: Pan Books, 1989.

Ehrlich, Dimitri. *Inside the Music: Conversations with Contemporary Musicians about Spirituality, Creativity, and Consciousness*. Boston: Shambhala, 1997.

Ensminger, David. *Left of the Dial: Conversations with Punk Icons*. Oakland, California: PM Press, 2013.

Ewen, David. *Dictators of the Baton*. Chicago: Ziff-Davis Publishing Company, 1948.

Ewen, David. *Famous Instrumentalists*. New York: Dodd, Mead & Company, 1965.

Finck, Henry T. *My Adventures in the Golden Age of Music*. New York and London: Funk & Wagnalls Company, 1926.

Finletter, Gretchen. *From the Top of the Stairs*. Boston, Massachusetts: Little, Brown and Company, 1946.

Friedman, Kinky. *'Scuse Me While I Whip This Out*. New York: Harper, 2004.

Frist, Karyn McLaughlin, editor. *"Love you, Daddy Boy": Daughters Honor the Fathers They Love*. Lanham, MD: Taylor Trade Publishing, 2006.

Goldsmith, Joan Oliver. *How Can We Keep from Singing: Music and the Passionate Life*. New York and London: W.W. Norton & Company, 2001.

Goode, Coleridge, and Roger Cotterrell. *Bass Lines: A Life in Jazz*. London: Northway Publications, 2002.

Govan, Chloe, *Taylor Swift: The Rise of the Nashville Teen*. London Omnibus Press, 2012.

Greenberg, Keith Elliot. *Rap*. Minneapolis, MN: Lerner Publications Company, 1988.

Hampton, Wilborn. *Elvis Presley: A Twentieth-Century Life*. New York: Viking, 2007.

Hemphill, Paul. *Lovesick Blues: The Life of Hank Williams*. New York: Penguin, 2005.

Henry, Lewis C. *Humorous Anecdotes About Famous People*. Garden City, NY: Halcyon House, 1948.

Hinton, Milt, David G. Berger, and Holly Maxson. *OverTime: The Jazz Photographs of Milt Hinton*. San Francisco, CA: Pomegranate Artbooks, 1991.

Horne, Marilyn. *Marilyn Horne: My Life*. With Jane Scovell. New York: Atheneum, 1983.

Jampol, Joshua. *Living Opera*. Oxford: Oxford University Press, 2010.

Jesella, Kara, and Marisa Melitzer. *How SASSY Changed My Life. A Love Letter to the Greatest Teen Magazine of All Time*. New York: Faber and Faber, Inc., 2007.

Johanson, Paula. *Lady Gaga: A Biography*. Santa Barbara, California: Greenwood, 2012.

Jones, Mrs. George, and Tom Carter. *Nashville Wives*. New York: HarperCollins*Publishers*, 1999.

Juno, Andrea. *Angry Women in Rock: Volume One*. New York: Juno Books, 1996.

Juno, Andrea, and V. Vale, publishers and editors. *Pranks! Devious Deeds and Mischievous Mirth*. San Francisco, CA: Re/Search Publications, 1987.

Kinney, Jack. *Walt Disney and Other Assorted Characters: An Unauthorized Account of the Early Years at Disney's*. New York: Harmony Books, 1988.

Kliment, Bud. *Count Basie*. Philadelphia, Pennsylvania: Chelsea House, 1992.

Kliment, Bud. *Ella Fitzgerald*. Philadelphia, Pennsylvania: Chelsea House Publishers, 1988.

Krohn, Katherine. *Ella Fitzgerald: First Lady of Song*. Minneapolis, Minnesota: Lerner Publications Company, 2001.

Lehmann, Lotte. *My Many Lives*. New York: Boosey & Hawkes Inc., 1948.

Lowe, Jacques. *Jazz: Photographs of the Masters*. New York: Artisan, 1995.

Markel, Rita J. *Jimi Hendrix*. Minneapolis, Minnesota: Lerner Publications Company, 2001.

Marshall, Jim. *Not Fade Away: The Rock & Roll Photographs of Jim Marshall*. Boston, MA: Little, Brown and Company, 1997.

Masar, Brenden. *The History of Punk Rock*. Detroit, MI: Lucent Publishing, 2006.

McCormack, Lily. *I Hear You Calling Me*. Milwaukee, Wisconsin: The Bruce Publishing Company, 1949.

McGuire, Jim. *Nashville Portraits: Sixty Portraits*. Guilford, Connecticut: The Lyons Press, 2007.

McMahon, Ed. *For Laughing Out Loud: My Life and Good Times*. With David Fisher. New York: Warner Books, Inc., 1998.

McMahon, Ed. *Here's Johnny! My Memories of Johnny Carson,* The Tonight Show, *and 46 Years of Friendship*. Nashville, TN: Rutledge Hill Press, 2005.

Melba, Nellie. *Melodies and Memories*. New York: George H. Doran Company, 1926.

Melnick, Monte A., and Frank Meyer. *On the Road with the Ramones*. London: Sanctuary Publishing, Limited, 2003.

Meltzer, Marisa. *Girl Power: The Nineties Revolution in Music*. New York: Faber and Faber, Inc., 2010.

Monem, Nadine, editor. *Riot Grrrl: Revolution Girl Style Now!* London: Black Dog Publishing, 2007.

Monteux, Fifi. *Everyone is Someone*. New York: Farrar, Straus and Cudahy, 1962.

Moore, Dudley. *Musical Bumps*. London: Robson Books, 1986.

Moore, Gerald. *Am I Too Loud? Memoirs of an Accompanist*. London: Hamish Hamilton, 1979.

Morrissey, James W. *Noted Men and Women*. New York: The Klebold Press, 1910.

Mostel, Kate, and Madeline Gilford. *170 Years of Show Business*. With Jack Gilford and Zero Mostel. New York: Random House, 1978.

Norkin, Sam. *Drawings, Stories: Theater, Opera, Ballet, Movies*. Portsmouth, NH: Heinemann, 1994.

O'Day, Anita. *High Times, Hard Times*. With George Eells. New York: Proscenium Publishers, Inc., 1989.

Pappas, Rita. *Barbra Streisand*. Philadelphia, Pennsylvania: Chelsea House Publishers, 2001.

Peck, Donald. *The Right Time, The Right Place! Tales of Chicago Symphony Days*. Bloomington and Indianapolis, IN: Indiana University Press, 2007.

Phillips, Julien. *Stars of the Ziegfeld Follies*. Minneapolis, MN: Lerner Publications Company, 1972.

Pollock, Bruce. *Interviews with Great Contemporary Songwriters*. Port Chester, NY: Cherry Lane Books, 1986.

Powell, Phelan. *Hanson*. Philadelphia, PA: Chelsea House Publishers, 1999.

Raphael, Amy. *Grrrls: Viva Rock Divas*. New York: St. Martin's Griffin, 1996.

Reich, Susanna. *Clara Schumann: Piano Virtuoso*. New York: Clarion Books, 1999.

Reisfeld, Randi. *Debbie Gibson: Electric Star*. New York: Bantam Books, 1990.

Rogers, Clara Kathleen (Clara Doria). *Memories of a Musical Career*. Norwood, Massachusetts: The Plimpton Press, 1932.

Rollins, Henry. *Get in the Van: On the Road with Black Flag*. Los Angeles, CA: 2.13.61, 2004.

Rossi, Melissa. *Courtney Love: Queen of Noise*. New York: Pocket Books, 1996.

Rubin, Susan Goldman. *Music was It: Young Leonard Bernstein*. Watertown, Massachusetts: Charlesbridge, 2011.

Schiedt, Duncan. *Jazz in Black and White*. Bloomington and Indianapolis, IN: Indiana University Press, 2004.

Schwarzkopf, Elisabeth. *On and Off the Record: A Memoir of Walter Legge*. New York: Charles Scribner's Sons, 1982.

Sellers, Michael, and Gary Morecambe. *Sellers on Sellers*. Additional material by Maxine Ventham. Great Britain: Andre Deutsch, 2000.

Sheen, Barbara. *Kanye West*. Detroit, Michigan: Lucent Books, 2010.

Shore, Nancy. *The Spice Girls*. Philadelphia, PA: Chelsea House Publishers, 1999.

Sills, Beverly. *Bubbles: A Self-Portrait*. Indianapolis, IN, and New York: Bobbs-Merrill, 1976.

Singer, Marilyn. *Cats to the Rescue*. New York: Henry Holt and Company, 2006.

Slezak, Walter. *What Time's the Next Swan?* Garden City, NY: Doubleday and Co., Inc., 1962.

Slonimsky, Nicolas. *Slonimsky's Book of Musical Anecdotes*. New York and London: Routledge, 2002.

Stauffer, Stacey L. *Garth Brooks*. Philadelphia, PA: Chelsea House Publishers, 2000.

Swenson, John. *Stevie Wonder*. London, England: Plexus Publishing Limited, 1986.

Tanner, Stephen. *Opera Antics and Anecdotes*. Toronto, Canada: Sound and Vision, 1999.

Thigpen, David E. *Jam Master Jay: The Heart of Hip Hop*. New York: Pocket Star Books, 2003.

Tosches, Nick. *Unsung Heroes of Rock 'n' Roll: The Birth of Rock 'n' Roll in the Dark and Wild Years Before Elvis*. New York: Charles Scribner's Sons, 1984.

Tracy, Kathleen. *Home Brewed: The Drew Carey Story*. New York: Boulevard Books, 1997.

Traubel, Helen. *St. Louis Woman*. New York: Duell, Sloan and Pearce, 1959.

True, Everett. *Hey Ho Let's Go: The Story of the Ramones*. London: Omnibus Press, 2002.

Turing, Penelope. *Hans Hotter, Man and Artist*. London: John Calder, 1983. Foreword by Sir Georg Solti.

Turner, Alwyn W. *Halfway to Paradise: The Birth of British Rock*. Photographs by Harry Hammond from the V&A Collection. London: V&A Publishing, 2008.

Ulrich, Homer. *Famous Women Singers*. New York: Dodd, Mead & Company, 1953.

Vale, V. and Andrea Juno, editors. *Incredibly Strange Music*. San Francisco: Re/Search Publications, 1993.

Vale, V., and Andrea Juno, editors. *Incredibly Strange Music, Vol. 2*. San Francisco, CA: Re/Search Publications, 1994.

Walker, Gerald, editor. *My Most Memorable Christmas*. New York: Pocket Books, Inc., 1963.

Wells, Steven. *Punk: Young, Loud, and Snotty*. New York: Thunder's Mouth Press, 2004.

Ybarra, T.R. *Caruso: The Man of Naples and the Voice of God*. New York: Harcourt, Brace and Company, 1953.

Zuckerman, Andrew. *Wisdom*. Edited by Alex Vlack. New York: Harry N. Abrams, Inc., 2008.

Zymet, Cathy Alter. *LeAnn Rimes*. Philadelphia, PA: Chelsea House Publishers, 1999.

Appendix B: About the Author

It was a dark and stormy night. Suddenly a cry rang out, and on a hot summer night in 1954, Josephine, wife of Carl Bruce, gave birth to a boy — me. Unfortunately, this young married couple allowed Reuben Saturday, Josephine's brother, to name their first-born. Reuben, aka "The Joker," decided that Bruce was a nice name, so he decided to name me Bruce Bruce. I have gone by my middle name — David — ever since.

Being named Bruce David Bruce hasn't been all bad. Bank tellers remember me very quickly, so I don't often have to show an ID. It can be fun in charades, also. When I was a counselor as a teenager at Camp Echoing Hills in Warsaw, Ohio, a fellow counselor gave the signs for "sounds like" and "two words," then she pointed to a bruise on her leg twice. Bruise Bruise? Oh yeah, Bruce Bruce is the answer!

Uncle Reuben, by the way, gave me a haircut when I was in kindergarten. He cut my hair short and shaved a small bald spot on the back of my head. My mother wouldn't let me go to school until the bald spot grew out again.

Of all my brothers and sisters (six in all), I am the only transplant to Athens, Ohio. I was born in Newark, Ohio, and have lived all around Southeastern Ohio. However, I moved to Athens to go to Ohio University and have never left.

At Ohio U, I never could make up my mind whether to major in English or Philosophy, so I got a bachelor's degree with a double major in both areas, then I added a Master of Arts degree in English and a Master of Arts degree in Philosophy. Yes, I have my MAMA degree.

Currently, and for a long time to come (I eat fruits and veggies), I am spending my retirement writing books such as *Nadia Comaneci: Perfect 10*, *The Funniest People in Comedy*, *Homer's* Iliad: *A Retelling in Prose*, and *William Shakespeare's* Hamlet: *A Retelling in Prose*.

By the way, my sister Brenda Kennedy writes romances such as *A New Beginning* and *Shattered Dreams*.

Appendix C: Some Books by David Bruce

Anecdote Collections

250 Anecdotes About Opera

250 Anecdotes About Religion

250 Anecdotes About Religion: Volume 2

250 Music Anecdotes

Be a Work of Art: 250 Anecdotes and Stories

The Coolest People in Art: 250 Anecdotes

The Coolest People in the Arts: 250 Anecdotes

The Coolest People in Books: 250 Anecdotes

The Coolest People in Comedy: 250 Anecdotes

Create, Then Take a Break: 250 Anecdotes

Don't Fear the Reaper: 250 Anecdotes

The Funniest People in Art: 250 Anecdotes

The Funniest People in Books: 250 Anecdotes

The Funniest People in Books, Volume 2: 250 Anecdotes

The Funniest People in Books, Volume 3: 250 Anecdotes

The Funniest People in Comedy: 250 Anecdotes

The Funniest People in Dance: 250 Anecdotes

The Funniest People in Families: 250 Anecdotes

The Funniest People in Families, Volume 2: 250 Anecdotes

The Funniest People in Families, Volume 3: 250 Anecdotes

The Funniest People in Families, Volume 4: 250 Anecdotes

The Funniest People in Families, Volume 5: 250 Anecdotes

The Funniest People in Families, Volume 6: 250 Anecdotes

The Funniest People in Movies: 250 Anecdotes

The Funniest People in Music: 250 Anecdotes

The Funniest People in Music, Volume 2: 250 Anecdotes

The Funniest People in Music, Volume 3: 250 Anecdotes

The Funniest People in Neighborhoods: 250 Anecdotes

The Funniest People in Relationships: 250 Anecdotes

The Funniest People in Sports: 250 Anecdotes

The Funniest People in Sports, Volume 2: 250 Anecdotes

The Funniest People in Television and Radio: 250 Anecdotes

The Funniest People in Theater: 250 Anecdotes

The Funniest People Who Live Life: 250 Anecdotes
The Funniest People Who Live Life, Volume 2: 250 Anecdotes
The Kindest People Who Do Good Deeds, Volume 1: 250 Anecdotes
The Kindest People Who Do Good Deeds, Volume 2: 250 Anecdotes
Maximum Cool: 250 Anecdotes
The Most Interesting People in Movies: 250 Anecdotes
The Most Interesting People in Politics and History: 250 Anecdotes
The Most Interesting People in Politics and History, Volume 2: 250 Anecdotes
The Most Interesting People in Politics and History, Volume 3: 250 Anecdotes
The Most Interesting People in Religion: 250 Anecdotes
The Most Interesting People in Sports: 250 Anecdotes
The Most Interesting People Who Live Life: 250 Anecdotes
The Most Interesting People Who Live Life, Volume 2: 250 Anecdotes
Reality is Fabulous: 250 Anecdotes and Stories
Resist Psychic Death: 250 Anecdotes
Seize the Day: 250 Anecdotes and Stories

[1] Source: Homer Ulrich, *Famous Women Singers*, pp. 63-64.

[2] Source: Everett True, *Hey Ho Let's Go: The Story of the Ramones*, pp. 7, 9.

[3] Source: Randi Reisfeld, *Debbie Gibson: Electric Star*, pp. 1, 4-5, 7-8.

[4] Source: Posts by Harriet Doorstop and Kathleen. Bikini Kill Archive. <http://bikinikillarchive.wordpress.com/>. Accessed on 11 March 2011.

[5] Source: Ann Angel, *Janis Joplin: Rise Up Singing*, pp. vii, 38, 64-65, 75, 94. Also: "Melisma." *The Free Dictionary*. <http://www.thefreedictionary.com/melisma>. Accessed 6 October 2013.

[6] Source: Gretchen Finletter, *From the Top of the Stairs*, pp. 4-9.

[7] Source: Simon Hattenstone, "Glen Campbell: One last love song." *Guardian* (UK). 26 August 2011 <http://www.guardian.co.uk/music/2011/aug/26/glen-campbell-interview>.

[8] Source: Melissa Rossi, *Courtney Love: Queen of Noise*, p. 51.

[9] Source: Lewis C. Henry, *Humorous Anecdotes About Famous People*, p. 83.

[10] Source: Jim Bessman, *Ramones: An American Band*, p. 160.

[11] Source: Craig McLean, "Why Stornoway are Britain's most exciting nu-folk band. Times Online. 7 May 2010 <http://entertainment.timesonline.co.uk/tol/arts_and_entertainment/music/article7118151.ece>.

[12] Source: Marilyn Singer, *Cats to the Rescue*, pp. 95-96.

[13] Source: Henry Rollins, *Get in the Van: On the Road with Black Flag*, pp. 45, 159-60, 295.

[14] Source: Joshua Jampol, *Living Opera*, pp. 57-58.

[15] Source: Christopher Borrelli, "Jim Peterik has been a rock star for decades, and he's not about to change now." *Chicago Tribune*. 30 August 2010 <http://www.popmatters.com/pm/article/130368-jim-peterik-has-been-a-rock-star-for-decades-and-hes-not-about-to-ch/>.

[16] Source: Stephen Tanner, *Opera Antics and Anecdotes*, p. 38.

[17] Source: Everett True, "Ten myths about grunge, Nirvana and Kurt Cobain." *Guardian (UK)*. 24 August 2011 <http://www.guardian.co.uk/music/2011/aug/24/grunge-myths-nirvana-kurt-cobain>.

[18] Source: Anita O'Day, *High Times, Hard Times*, p. 109.

[19] Source: Ed McMahon, *For Laughing Out Loud: My Life and Good Times*, p. 250.

[20] Source: Alwyn W. Turner, *Halfway to Paradise: The Birth of British Rock*, pp. 132, 134.

[21] Source: Nick Tosches, *Unsung Heroes of Rock 'n' Roll: The Birth of Rock 'n' Roll in the Dark and Wild Years Before Elvis*, p. 41.

[22] Source: Dave Steinfeld, "When Everything Cliks." Curvemag.com. 24 September 2009 <http://www.curvemag.com/Curve-Magazine/Web-Articles-2008/When-Everything-Cliks/>.

[23] Source: Andrea Juno, *Angry Women in Rock: Volume One*, p. 36.

[24] Source: Donald Brook, *Singers of Today*, p. 118.

[25] Source: Pete Paphides, "Billy Bragg: still barking at injustice." Timesonline.co.uk. 19 February 2010 <http://entertainment.timesonline.co.uk/tol/arts_and_entertainment/music/article7032305.ece>.

[26] Source: Rita Pappas, *Barbra Streisand*, pp. 14-15, 19.

[27] Source: Joshua Jampol, *Living Opera*, pp. 64-65.

[28] Source: Will Harris, "A Chat with Corey Glover, Living Colour singer." Bullz-eye.com. 8 October 2009 <http://www.bullz-eye.com/music/interviews/2009/corey_glover.htm>.

[29] Source: Chris Ayres, "Black Sabbath recall birth of heavy metal on its 40th anniversary." *The Times.* 13 February 2010 <http://entertainment.timesonline.co.uk/tol/arts_and_entertainment/article7025742.ece>.

[30] Source: Angelica Shirley Carpenter and Jean Shirley, *Robert Louis Stevenson: Finding Treasure Island*, pp. 106, 109.

[31] Source: Amy Raphael, *Grrrls: Viva Rock Divas*, pp. 64, 72.

[32] Source: Gladys Burch and John Wolcott, *Famous Composers for Young People*, pp. 12-13, 21-22, 36, 40, 73-75, 106, 150, 153-154.

[33] Source: John Swenson, *Stevie Wonder*, pp. 7, 10, 12, 40, 42.

[34] Source: Susanna Reich, *Clara Schumann: Piano Virtuoso*, pp. 19, 22-23, 26, 95.

[35] Source: Joan Oliver Goldsmith, *How Can We Keep from Singing: Music and the Passionate Life*, pp. 43, 49, 96.

[36] Source: Cathy Alter Zymet, *LeAnn Rimes*, pp. 8, 18-19, 22.

[37] Source: Karyn McLaughlin Frist, editor, *"Love you, Daddy Boy": Daughters Honor the Fathers They Love*, p. 72.

[38] Source: Phelan Powell, *Hanson*, pp. 19, 54.

[39] Source: Victoria Balfour, *Rock Wives*, pp. 53-54.

[40] Source: James W. Morrissey, *Noted Men and Women*, p. 38.

[41] Source: Gerald Walker, editor, *My Most Memorable Christmas*, p. 122.

[42] Source: Bruce Dessau, *George Michael: The Making of a Superstar*, pp. 65, 178.

[43] Source: Paula Johanson, *Lady Gaga: A Biography*, pp. 20-21.

[44] Source: Gerald Walker, editor, *My Most Memorable Christmas*, pp. 16-17.

[45] Source: Mrs. George Jones and Tom Carter, *Nashville Wives*, pp. 168-69.

[46] Source: David E. Thigpen, *Jam Master Jay: The Heart of Hip Hop*, pp. 143-144.

[47] Source: "Heidi's Christmas present to her boss." Photos — Henry Rollins." <http://henryrollins.com/photo/heidis_christmas_present_to_her_boss/>. Accessed 9 January 2011. Also: "PUBLIC SERVICE ANNOUNCEMENT RE: HENRY ROLLINS AND HEIDI MAY." <http://www.hellohenry.com/2008/03/25/public-service-announcement-re-henry-rollins-heidi-may/>. Accessed 9 January 2011.

[48] Source: Anita O'Day, *High Times, Hard Times*, pp. 101-102.

[49] Source: Lisa Verrico, "Why Scouting for Girls lay low." *Sunday Times*. 14 March 2010 <http://entertainment.timesonline.co.uk/tol/arts_and_entertainment/music/article7056788.ece>.

[50] Source: Mina Carson, Tisa Lewis, and Susan M. Shaw, *Girls Rock! Fifty Years of Women Making Music*, p. 111.

[51] Source: Jack Benny and His Daughter Joan, *Sunday Nights at Seven: The Jack Benny Story*, pp. 235, 289.

[52] Source: Andrew Purcell, "Steve Martin – a man with two reigns." *Guardian*. 26 May 2011 <http://www.guardian.co.uk/culture/2011/may/26/steve-martin-bluegrass-banjo>.

[53] Source: Ed McMahon, *For Laughing Out Loud: My Life and Good Times*, pp. 182-183.

[54] Source: Kate Mostel and Madeline Gilford, *170 Years of Show Business*, p. 93.

[55] Source: Penelope Turing, *Hans Hotter, Man and Artist*, pp. 86-87, 247.

[56] Source: Lily McCormack, *I Hear You Calling Me*, pp. 136-137.

[57] Source: Coleridge Goode and Roger Cotterrell, *Bass Lines: A Life in Jazz*, pp. 147-148.

[58] Source: Gretchen Finletter, *From the Top of the Stairs*, pp. 196-197.

[59] Source: Samuel Antek, *This was Toscanini*, pp. 130, 134.

[60] Source: Elisabeth Schwarzkopf, *On and Off the Record: A Memoir of Walter Legge*, pp. 223-234.

[61] Source: Walter Damrosch, *My Musical Life*, pp. 88-89.

[62] Source: Elisabeth Schwarzkopf, *On and Off the Record: A Memoir of Walter Legge*, pp. 152-153.

[63] Source: Walter Slezak, *What Time's the Next Swan?*, p. 32.

[64] Source: Fifi Monteux, *Everyone is Someone*, p. 63.

[65] Source: David Blum, *Quintet: Five Journeys Toward Musical Fulfillment*, pp. 92-93.

[66] Source: Helen Traubel, *St. Louis Woman*, p. 180.

[67] Source: David Blum, *Quintet: Five Journeys Toward Musical Fulfillment*, p. 70.

[68] Source: David Ewen, *Dictators of the Baton*, pp. 63-64.

[69] Source: Josh Gross: "Don't Listen Here: Nickelback, June 13, Idaho Center." *Boise Weekly* (Idaho). 6 June 2012 <http://www.boiseweekly.com/boise/dont-listen-here/Content?oid=2662087>.

[70] Source: David L. Ulin, "Neil Young's Memoir, Waging Heavy Peace, Offers a Wandering Glimpse of His Life and Music." *Los Angeles Times* (California). 8 November 2012 <http://www.popmatters.com/pm/wire/165230-waging-heavy-peace-a-hippie-dream/>.

[71] Source: Lotte Lehmann, *My Many Lives*, p. 95

[72] Source: Nicolas Slonimsky, *Slonimsky's Book of Musical Anecdotes*, pp. 120-121.

[73] Source: Marilyn Horne, *Marilyn Horne: My Life*, pp. 120-121.

[74] Source: Laura Barnett, "Portrait of the artist: Marin Alsop, conductor." *Guardian* (UK). 14 June 2010 <http://www.guardian.co.uk/culture/2010/jun/14/marin-alsop-conductor>.

[75] Source: Beverly Sills, *Bubbles: A Self-Portrait*, p. 214.

[76] Source: Lily McCormack, *I Hear You Calling Me*, pp. 137-138.

[77] Source: Joey Adams, *The God Bit*, p. 320.

[78] Source: Bud Kliment, *Ella Fitzgerald*, pp. 35-36, 40, 56-57.

[79] Source: Karl Böhm, *A Life Remembered: Memoirs*, pp. 28-29.

[80] Source: Johnny Davis, "Quincy Jones: 'I knew how to handle Michael.'" *Guardian* (UK). 8 September 2010 <http://www.guardian.co.uk/music/2010/sep/08/quincy-jones>.

[81] Source: Roger Ebert, "What do you mean by a miracle?" Blogs.suntimes.com 14 October 2010 <http://blogs.suntimes.com/ebert/2010/10/post_3.html>.

[82] Source: Gladys Burch and John Wolcott, *Famous Composers for Young People*, pp. 81-85, 92.

[83] Source: Brian Braiker, "London 2012 organisers wanted Keith Moon to play at Olympics ceremony: Drummer died from a drug overdose in 1978 at the age of 32." *Guardian* (UK). 13 April 2012 <http://www.guardian.co.uk/music/us-news-blog/2012/apr/13/keith-moon-london-olympics-organisers>.

[84] Source: V. Vale and Andrea Juno, editors, *Incredibly Strange Music*, pp. 55-58, 61, 65.

[85] Source: "R. Crumb, The Art of Comics No. 1": Interviewed by Ted Widmer. *The Paris Review*. 2010 <http://www.theparisreview.org/interviews/6017/the-art-of-comics-no-1-r-crumb>.

[86] Source: V. Vale and Andrea Juno, editors, *Incredibly Strange Music, Vol. 2*, pp. 29, 31, 37, 50.

[87] Source: Andrea Juno, *Angry Women in Rock: Volume One*, pp.136-137.

[88] Source: Ana Samways, "June 6: Wheelie bin love." *Sideswipe. New Zealand Herald*. 6 June 2012 <http://www.nzherald.co.nz/ana-samways/news/article.cfm?a_id=53&objectid=10810964>.

[89] Source: Susan Goldman Rubin, *Music was It: Young Leonard Bernstein*, pp. 67, 81, 85, 87.

[90] Source: Clara Kathleen Rogers (Clara Doria), *Memories of a Musical Career*, pp. 120-123, 127.

[91] Source: Andrew Zuckerman, *Wisdom*, p. 26.

[92] Source: Wilborn Hampton, *Elvis Presley: A Twentieth-Century Life*, pp. 31, 38.

[93] Source: Byron Janis, "Nurturing Creativity in the Next Generation." *Wall Street Journal*. 8 December 2010 <http://online.wsj.com/art."le/SB10001424052748703514904575602772971252634.html?mod=WSJ_LifeStyle_Lifest

[94] Source: Jude Rogers, "Schoolteachers of rock." *Guardian* (UK). 25 April 2010 <http://www.guardian.co.uk/music/2010/apr/25/inspirational-music-teachers>.

[95] Source: Mark Stryker, "Jazz saxophonist James Moody plays on." *Detroit Free Press*. 15 January 2010 <http://www.popmatters.com/pm/article/119066-jazz-saxophonist-james-moody-plays-on/>.

[96] Source: Fifi Monteux, *Everyone is Someone*, pp. 114-115.

[97] Source: T.R. Ybarra, *Caruso: The Man of Naples and the Voice of God*, p 162.

[98] Source: Amy Raphael, *Grrrls: Viva Rock Divas*, pp. 4, 16, 30.

[99] Source: Donald Peck, *The Right Time, The Right Place! Tales of Chicago Symphony Days*, p. 62.

[100] Source: Catherine Rapley, "This much I know: Paolo Nutini, singer, 22, London." *Guardian* (UK). 23 August 2009 <http://www.guardian.co.uk/lifeandstyle/2009/aug/23/paolo-nutini-this-much-know>.

[101] Source: Anne K. Brown, *Katy Perry*, pp. 16, 18-19, 25, 34, 36, 47-48, 76.

[102] Source: Victoria Balfour, *Rock Wives*, pp. 125, 128, 133-34.

[103] Source: David Aretha, *Awesome African-American Rock and Soul Musicians*, pp. 79-81, 85.

[104] Source: Laura Barnett, "Portrait of the artist: Rufus Wainwright, musician." *Guardian (UK)*. 12 April 2010 <http://www.guardian.co.uk/culture/2010/apr/12/rufus-wainwright-musician>.

[105] Source: Stacey L. Stauffer, *Garth Brooks*, pp. 9-10, 14.

[106] Source: Joan Oliver Goldsmith, *How Can We Keep from Singing: Music and the Passionate Life*, pp. 87-88.

[107] Source: Richard Clayton, "Groening adds more strings to his d'oh." *The Sunday Times*. 25 April 2010 <http://entertainment.timesonline.co.uk/tol/arts_and_entertainment/music/article7104059.ece>.

[108] Source: Wilborn Hampton, *Elvis Presley: A Twentieth-Century Life*, pp. 13, 18-19.

[109] Source: Monte A. Melnick and Frank Meyer, *On the Road with the Ramones*, p. 266.

[110] Source: Duncan Schiedt, *Jazz in Black and White*, pp. 6-7.

[111] Source: Kara Jesella and Marisa Melitzer, *How SASSY Changed My Life. A Love Letter to the Greatest Teen Magazine of All Time*, p. 47.

[112] Source: "ATC-I'm In Heaven (When You Kiss Me) Lyrics." YouTube.com. <http://www.youtube.com/watch?v=mtXlRuZ-A2E&feature=related>. Accessed on 12 April 2011.

[113] Source: Katie Couric, *The Best Advice I Ever Got: Lessons from Extraordinary Lives*, p. 96.

[114] Source: Tim Teeman, "Tori Amos: 'Anything is easier to talk about in music than in conversation.'" *Guardian*. 15 September 2013 <http://www.theguardian.com/music/2013/sep/15/tori-amos-interview>.

[115] Source: Walter Damrosch, *My Musical Life*, p. 79.

[116] Source: Karyn McLaughlin Frist, editor, *"Love you, Daddy Boy": Daughters Honor the Fathers They Love*, p. 28.

[117] Source: Sam Norkin, *Drawings, Stories*, p. 88.

[118] Source: Dimitri Ehrlich, *Inside the Music: Conversations with Contemporary Musicians about Spirituality, Creativity, and Consciousness*, pp. 98, 100.

[119] Source: Zora von Burden, editor, *Women of the Underground: Music*, p. 99.

[120] Source: Randi Reisfeld, *Debbie Gibson: Electric Star*, p. 6.

[121] Source: David E. Thigpen, *Jam Master Jay: The Heart of Hip Hop*, p. 101.

[122] Source: Lewis C. Henry, *Humorous Anecdotes About Famous People*, pp. 145-150.

[123] Source: James W. Morrissey, *Noted Men and Women*, pp. 39-41.

[124] Source: Rita J. Markel, *Jimi Hendrix*, pp. 18-19, 23-25, 39-40, 88.

[125] Source: Susan Goldman Rubin, *Music was It: Young Leonard Bernstein*, pp. 60, 78, 143-144.

[126] Source: Kinky Friedman, *'Scuse Me While I Whip This Out*, pp. 7, 21.

[127] Source: Jacques Lowe, *Jazz: Photographs of the Masters*, pp. 180-181.

[128] Source: Nellie Melba, *Melodies and Memories*, pp. 194-196.

[129] Source: Milt Hinton, David G. Berger, and Holly Maxson, *OverTime: The Jazz Photographs of Milt Hinton*, p. 68.

[130] Source: Nancy Shore, *The Spice Girls*, pp. 31, 33-34.

[131] Source: Sam Leith, "The unstoppable rise of Russell Brand." *Guardian (UK)*. 6 April 2010 <http://www.guardian.co.uk/media/2010/apr/06/russell-brand>.

[132] Source: Henry Rollins, *Get in the Van: On the Road with Black Flag*, pp. 12-13, 97, 131, 147.

[133] Source: Bud Kliment, *Count Basie*, pp. 52, 68-69, 110.

[134] Source: Paul Hemphill, *Lovesick Blues: The Life of Hank Williams*, pp. 67-68, 78.

[135] Source: Iain Aitch, "The Ex: experimental noiseniks." *Guardian (UK)*. 21 January 2010 http://www.guardian.co.uk/music/2010/jan/21/the-ex-interview.

[136] Source: Jim Marshall, *Not Fade Away: The Rock & Roll Photographs of Jim Marshall*, p. 61.

[137] Source: Chloe Govan, *Taylor Swift: The Rise of the Nashville Teen*, pp. 51-52.

[138] Source: David Ewen, *Famous Instrumentalists*, pp. 25, 27.

[139] Source: Ed McMahon, *Here's Johnny! My Memories of Johnny Carson, The Tonight Show, and 46 Years of Friendship*, p. 141.

[140] Source: Helen Traubel, *St. Louis Woman*, p. 47.

[141] Source: Mrs. George Jones and Tom Carter, *Nashville Wives*, pp. 42-43.

[142] Source: *Too Tough to Die: A Tribute to Johnny Ramone*, a documentary.

[143] Source: Ed McMahon, *Here's Johnny! My Memories of Johnny Carson, The Tonight Show, and 46 Years of Friendship*, pp. 203-206.

[144] Source: Monte A. Melnick and Frank Meyer, *On the Road with the Ramones*, pp. 142, 258.

[145] Source: Richard Barthelemy, *Memories of Caruso*, pp. 9-10.

[146] Source: Henry T. Finck, *My Adventures in the Golden Age of Music*, pp. 310-311.

[147] Source: Samuel Antek, *This was Toscanini*, pp. 89-91, 102.

[148] Source: David Ewen, *Dictators of the Baton*, p. 45.

[149] Source: Ginny Dougary, "Leonard Bernstein, the father I knew." *The Times*. 13 March 2010 <http://entertainment.timesonline.co.uk/tol/arts_and_entertainment/music/classical/article7059407.ece>.

[150] Source: Duncan Schiedt, *Jazz in Black and White*, pp. 24-25.

[151] Source: Scott Saul, "Review of *Thelonious Monk: The Life and Times of an American Original* by Robin D. G. Kelley." *Boston Review*. September/October 2010 <http://www.bostonreview.net/BR35.5/saul.php>.

[152] Source: Richard Barthelemy, *Memories of Caruso*, p. 9.

[153] Source: Nicolas Slonimsky, *Slonimsky's Book of Musical Anecdotes*, p. 206.

[154] Source: Alfred Hickling, "Emmylou Harris: 'I looked down on country.'" *Guardian*. 4 March 2012 <http://www.guardian.co.uk/music/2013/mar/04/emmylou-harris-looked-down-country>.

[155] Source: Beverly Sills, *Bubbles: A Self-Portrait*, pp. 113, 159, 198-199.

[156] Source: Chris Ayres, "Alice Cooper: booze, madness and chickens." *The Times*. 20 November 2009 <http://entertainment.timesonline.co.uk/tol/arts_and_entertainment/music/article6923831.ece>.

[157] Source: Brian Aberback, *Black Sabbath: Pioneers of Heavy Metal*, pp. 21, 67.

[158] Source: Gerald Moore, *Am I Too Loud? Memoirs of an Accompanist*, pp. 54-55, 140.

[159] Source: Laura Barnett, "Portrait of the artist: Cerys Matthews, singer." *Guardian (UK)*. 28 September 2009 <http://www.guardian.co.uk/culture/2009/sep/28/cerys-matthews-singer>.

[160] Source: Nellie Melba, *Melodies and Memories*, pp. 213-214.

[161] Source: Kinky Friedman, *'Scuse Me While I Whip This Out*, p. 100.

[162] Source: Victor Borge, *My Favorite Intervals*, pp. 109-110.

[163] Source: T.R. Ybarra, *Caruso: The Man of Naples and the Voice of God*, pp. 233-235, 237.

[164] Source: Henry Rollins, "Listening to Ramones in Tehran." *Los Angeles Weekly*. 10 March 2011 <http://blogs.laweekly.com/westcoastsound/2011/03/listening_to_ramones_in_tehran.php>.

[165] Source: Caitlin Moran, "Come party with Lady Gaga." *The Times*. May 2010 <http://entertainment.timesonline.co.uk/tol/arts_and_entertainment/music/article7129672.ece>.

[166] Source: Julien Phillips, *Stars of the Ziegfeld Follies*, p. 43.

[167] Source: Jack Benny and His Daughter Joan, *Sunday Nights at Seven: The Jack Benny Story*, pp. 226-227.

[168] Source: Karl Böhm, *A Life Remembered: Memoirs*, p. 44.

[169] Source: Clara Kathleen Rogers (Clara Doria), *Memories of a Musical Career*, pp. 320-321.

[170] Source: Mina Carson, Tisa Lewis, and Susan M. Shaw, *Girls Rock! Fifty Years of Women Making Music*, pp. 82-83.

[171] Source: Julia Blackburn, *With Billie: A New Look at the Unforgettable Lady Day*, pp. 84-85.

[172] Source: Ana Samways, "March 7: Building a little chicken." *Sideswipe*. *New Zealand Herald*. 7 March 2013 <http://www.nzherald.co.nz/sideswipe-with-ana-samways/news/article.cfm?c_id=1503050&objectid=10869650>.

[173] Source: "Divinyls: 'I Touch Myself.'" YouTube. <http://www.youtube.com/watch?v=n2YOtDMMpow>. Accessed on 5 May 2011.

[174] Source: Jim Bessman, *Ramones: An American Band*, pp. 146-147.

[175] Source: Erik Anjou, *Dave Matthews Band*, pp. 28-29, 33-37.

[176] Source: Barbara Sheen, *Kanye West*, pp. 17, 19, 22-23, 38-39, 74.

[177] Source: Neil Gaiman, "Neil Gaiman on Lou Reed: 'His songs were the soundtrack to my life.'" *Guardian*. 28 October 2013 <http://www.theguardian.com/music/2013/oct/28/neil-gaiman-lou-reed-sandman>.

[178] Source: Kara Jesella and Marisa Melitzer, *How SASSY Changed My Life. A Love Letter to the Greatest Teen Magazine of All Time*, pp. 48-49.

[179] Source: Alwyn W. Turner, *Halfway to Paradise: The Birth of British Rock*, pp. 118, 121.

[180] Source: Keith Elliot Greenberg, *Rap*, pp. 21, 27.

[181] Source: Marisa Meltzer, *Girl Power: The Nineties Revolution in Music*, pp. 4, 7-8, 26.

[182] Source: V. Vale and Andrea Juno, editors, *Incredibly Strange Music, Vol. 2*, pp. 76-77, 79-80.

[183] Source: Dimitri Ehrlich, *Inside the Music: Conversations with Contemporary Musicians about Spirituality, Creativity, and Consciousness*, pp. 75, 78-79.

[184] Source: Zora von Burden, editor, *Women of the Underground: Music*, pp. 164, 211.

[185] Source: Steven Wells, *Punk: Young, Loud, and Snotty*, p. 38.

[186] Source: V. Vale and Andrea Juno, editors, *Incredibly Strange Music*, pp. 108-110.

[187] Source: Milt Hinton, David G. Berger, and Holly Maxson, *OverTime: The Jazz Photographs of Milt Hinton*, p. 11.

[188] Source: Julia Blackburn, *With Billie: A New Look at the Unforgettable Lady Day*, p. 325.

[189] Source: Alex James, "Alex James on reuniting with Blur." *The Times*. 16 January 2010 <http://entertainment.timesonline.co.uk/tol/arts_and_entertainment/music/article6988355.ece>.

[190] Source: Andrea Juno and V. Vale, publishers and editors, *Pranks! Devious Deeds and Mischievous Mirth*, p. 63.

[191] Source: Peter Belsito and Bob Davis, *Hardcore California: A History of Punk and New Wave*, pp. 93, 106-107.

[192] Source: Katherine Krohn, *Ella Fitzgerald: First Lady of Song*, pp. 66, 68, 76, 81-82, 89-90, 92.

[193] Source: Henry T. Finck, *My Adventures in the Golden Age of Music*, p. 81.

[194] Source: Paul Hemphill, *Lovesick Blues: The Life of Hank Williams*, p. 99.

[195] Source: Walter Slezak, *What Time's the Next Swan?*, p. 211.

[196] Source: Donald Peck, *The Right Time, The Right Place! Tales of Chicago Symphony Days*, p. 74.

[197] Source: Stephen Tanner, *Opera Antics and Anecdotes*, p. 51.

[198] Source: Claudia Roth Pierpont, "BLACK, BROWN, AND BEIGE." *The New Yorker*. 17 May 2010 <http://www.newyorker.com/arts/critics/atlarge/2010/05/17/100517crat_atlarge_pierpont?currentPage=all>.

[199] Source: David Aretha, *Awesome African-American Rock and Soul Musicians*, pp. 13-14, 16, 18.

[200] Source: Interviews by Killian Fox, "NME: 60 years of rock history ... and four front covers that define their eras. *Guardian* (UK). 25 February 2012 <http://www.guardian.co.uk/music/2012/feb/26/nme-60-editors-favourite-covers>.

[201] Source: Alexis Petridis, "Bobby Womack: 'I can sing my ass off, better than I could before.'" *Guardian* (UK). 24 May 2012 <http://www.guardian.co.uk/music/2012/may/24/bobby-womack-sing-better-before>.

[202] Source: Homer Ulrich, *Famous Women Singers*, pp. 105-107.

[203] Source: Coleridge Goode and Roger Cotterrell, *Bass Lines: A Life in Jazz*, pp. 45-46, 166-67.

[204] Source: Sarah Caldwell, *Challenges: A Memoir of My Life in Opera*, pp. 52, 58-59.

[205] Source: Sarah Caldwell, *Challenges: A Memoir of My Life in Opera*, pp. 43-45.

[206] Source: Dave Steinfeld, "One on One with Anna Egge," *Curve Magazine*. Accessed 31 January 2010 <http://www.curvemag.com/Curve-Magazine/Web-Articles-2008/One-on-One-with-Anna-Egge/>.

[207] Source: Penelope Turing, *Hans Hotter, Man and Artist*, pp. 108-109.

[208] Source: Marilyn Horne, *Marilyn Horne: My Life*, p. 108.

[209] Source: Paula Johanson, *Lady Gaga: A Biography*, pp. 18, 28-29.

[210] Source: David Ensminger, *Left of the Dial: Conversations with Punk Icons*, pp. 120-121, 124-125. Also: "Ian MacKaye." Wikipedia. Accessed 13 January 2014 <http://en.wikipedia.org/wiki/Ian_MacKaye>.

[211] Source: Peter Belsito and Bob Davis, *Hardcore California: A History of Punk and New Wave*, pp. 15, 31, 36, 46, 80-81, 119.

[212] Source: Steven Wells, *Punk: Young, Loud, and Snotty*, pp. 35-37.

[213] Source: Brian J. Bowe, *The Ramones: American Punk Band*, pp. 28, 42-43, 68-69.

[214] Source: Brenden Masar, *The History of Punk Rock*, pp. 19, 43-44, 59.

[215] Source: Alexis Petridis, "Richard Hawley: Rock'n'roll troubadour." *Guardian (UK)*. 20 September 2009 <http://www.guardian.co.uk/music/2009/sep/20/richard-hawley-sheffield>.

[216] Source: Dudley Moore, *Musical Bumps*, p. 31.

[217] Source: Dudley Moore, *Musical Bumps*, p. 22.

[218] Source: Lotte Lehmann, *My Many Lives*, pp. 92-93.

[219] Source: Sam Norkin, *Drawings, Stories*, p. 303.

[220] Source: Donald Brook, *Singers of Today*, p. 154.

[221] Source: Cazz Blaze, "Poems on the Underground," pp. 77-79. Collected in this book: Nadine Monem, editor, *Riot Grrrl: Revolution Girl Style Now!*

[222] Source: Beth Ditto, "Foreword," p. 8. Nadine Monem, editor, *Riot Grrrl: Revolution Girl Style Now!*

[223] Source: Jim McGuire, *Nashville Portraits: Sixty Portraits*, pp. 36-37.

[224] Source: Bruce Pollock, *Interviews with Great Contemporary Songwriters*, p. 66.

[225] Source: Bruce Pollock, *Interviews with Great Contemporary Songwriters*, p. 29.

[226] Source: Andrew Zuckerman, *Wisdom*, p. 130.

[227] Source: Jim McGuire, *Nashville Portraits: Sixty Portraits*, pp. 38-39.

[228] Source: Bud Kliment, *Ella Fitzgerald*, pp. 14-18, 45-46, 99-100.

[229] Source: Kathleen Tracy, *Home Brewed: The Drew Carey Story*, pp. 84-85.

[230] Source: Gerald Moore, *Am I Too Loud? Memoirs of an Accompanist*, pp. 245, 261-262.

[231] Source: Michael Sellers and Gary Morecambe, *Sellers on Sellers*, p. 149.

[232] Source: John Swenson, *Stevie Wonder*, pp. 98-100.

[233] Source: David Ewen, *Famous Instrumentalists*, pp. 139-40, 144-45.

[234] Source: Emma Brockes, "Mariah Carey: 'I try not to be a jerk. I really do.'" *Guardian (UK)*. 3 October 2009 <http://www.guardian.co.uk/music/2009/oct/03/mariah-carey-interview>.

[235] Source: Marc Myers, "Who Else Made More Hit Songs?" *Wall Street Journal*. 23 March 2011 <http://online.wsj.com/article/SB10001424052748703858404576214574291829718.html?mod=WSJ_LifeStyle_Lifest

[236] Source: Stevie Chick, "Songs about Darwin: The Low Anthem." *Guardian (UK)*. 4 February 2010 <http://www.guardian.co.uk/music/2010/feb/04/low-anthem-charlie-darwin>.

[237] Source: Jude Rogers, "The wisdom of boybands." *Guardian (UK)*. 28 October 2009 <http://www.guardian.co.uk/music/2009/oct/28/boyband-take-that-westlife-blue>.

[238] Source: Chloe Govan, *Taylor Swift: The Rise of the Nashville Teen*, p. 88. Also Jerry Jean, "An Interview with Multi-Platinum Record Producer Steve Migliore, aka Mr. Mig." Musicianwages.com. 8 March 2010 <http://tinyurl.com/kzorxns>.

[239] Source: Jim Marshall, *Not Fade Away: The Rock & Roll Photographs of Jim Marshall*, p. 5.

[240] Source: Nick Tosches, *Unsung Heroes of Rock 'n' Roll: The Birth of Rock 'n' Roll in the Dark and Wild Years Before Elvis*, pp. 79-80.

[241] Source: Chip Deffaw, *Jazz Veterans: A Portrait Gallery*, p. 72.

[242] Source: Jack Kinney, *Walt Disney and Other Assorted Characters*, p. 84.

[243] Source: Stephen Brook, "Krissi Murison: 'I have always loved the chase of finding new bands.'" *Guardian (UK)*. 5 April 2010 <http://www.guardian.co.uk/media/2010/apr/05/krissi-murison-nme-editor-interview>.

[244] Source: Jacques Lowe, *Jazz: Photographs of the Masters*, pp. 68-69.

[245] Source: Everett True, *Hey Ho Let's Go: The Story of the Ramones*, p. 30.

[246] Source: Howard Reich, "Von Freeman, Chicago jazz legend, dead at 88." *Chicago Tribune* (Illinois). 15 August 2012 <http://www.popmatters.com/pm/wire/162152-von-freeman-chicago-jazz-legend-dead-at-88/>.

[247] Source: Chip Deffaw, *Jazz Veterans: A Portrait Gallery*, p. 80.

[248] Source: Victor Borge, *My Favorite Intervals*, p 141.

[249] Source: Dave Simpson, "Jack White on the Mississippi blues artists: 'They changed the world.'" *Guardian*. 7 March 2013 <http://www.guardian.co.uk/music/2013/mar/07/jack-white-blues-artists>.

[250] Source: Joey Adams, *The God Bit*, p. 87.

www.ingramcontent.com/pod-product-compliance
Lightning Source LLC
Chambersburg PA
CBHW031334160726
47993CB00002B/674